ALEX JARDINE

KU-575-419

To Mum

from her daughter.

October, 1958.

and again

December 1977.

HOW TO KEEP PACE WITH YOUR DAUGHTER

" Sane, normal and nineteen."

HOW TO KEEP PACE
WITH
YOUR DAUGHTER

By
ETHELIND FEARON

Author of
The Reluctant Gardener: The Reluctant Hostess:
The Reluctant Cook, etc.

pictured by
ALEX JARDINE

LONDON : HERBERT JENKINS

First published by
Herbert Jenkins Ltd.
3 Duke of York Street,
London, S.W.1.
1958

MADE AND PRINTED IN GREAT BRITAIN BY PURNELL AND SONS, LTD.
PAULTON (SOMERSET) AND LONDON

I got me flowers to straw thy way;
I got me boughs off many a tree:
But thou wast up by break of day,
And brought'st thy sweets along with thee.

GEORGE HERBERT

CONTENTS

I

Ways to a Common Wavelength

THE prospect of a desperate and out-dated mamma in hot pursuit of a fast daughter should ring all withers (wherever and whatever these may be). It is not only undignified, it is downright deplorable, but it is universally considered to be one of the penalties of advancing age.

Either you speed like mad to catch up with Offspring's headlong career or you give it up and lose touch with her. You will obviously sink from Today backwards into Yesterday, Last Year, and finally Last Generation with not a clue in the world as to what the child is up to.

Don't become a Study in Decline. If you do it's your own fault that nobody loves you. On the other hand beware of becoming too advanced. If there's one thing that gives me goose-pimples quicker than a sophistication of fast daughters hurtling hot-foot round, over or through all opposition, with their panting dams wallowing in the rear, it is a race of fast mammas well in the lead with daughters faint but pursuing.

Fortunately a slight application of subtlety can resolve this problem.

Nobody said it was a *race* did they? You forgot to ask how fast is *fast* or the pace of the pace, and with a little thought we can fix our mutual progress very agreeably to coincide, mutton and lamb gambolling gaily together.

To keep pace merely assumes that we shall be moving at the same speed, and preferably in the same direction. If you can, by early training, by present distractions and by future decoys so regulate her progress that she stops to pick flowers by the wayside or gather a little wool you can accompany her without loss of either breath or dignity and it will be less noticeable that you have accumulated considerable moss yourself. You can both proceed comfortably and even take pleasure in the association.

It is this latter state which we shall discuss presently, the methods of speeding-up the progress of the aged and controlling the impulses of the young so that they reach an optimum number of revolutions per minute and miles per hour which will be mutually becoming and beneficial.

If you can induce her to keep pace with *you*, it's automatic that you can keep pace with *her*. Only this time you will be the pacemaker without her knowledge.

There are many ways to this common wavelength, the easiest being to produce some object of common interest (an occupation, an entertainment, a man) and jointly study it. Though in the last case it is advisable that your own research in this field be not too intense.

One of the greatest single differences between young and old is that the former are still learning—expanding their mental and spiritual skin—and the old have ceased to learn and become ossified.

Once you regard yourself as complete—or even, in a purely negative way, cease to regard yourself at all, merely do nothing to augment your accomplishments—you are finished and well on the way to mummification.

How can you expect the young to walk beside you or even to have any means of communication with you, if you are closed and shell-bound, not a root or a tentacle sticking out anywhere with which to explore, no crack in your complacent hide through which they can reach you.

They can't talk to you if you're shut up in a shell—complete—perfect—finished, with all your thoughts turned inward. No wonder the Child seeks exclusively her contemporaries, as springy of mind and elastic of purpose and body as herself.

It's exercise that keeps you young.

And adaptability.

No-one is static. Or if they *are* they're dead, whether they know it or not. And the world's least static objects are the young. I'm afraid you'll have to adapt your daily outlook to match the ceaseless changes in them, in their background and in ourselves.

And if you can find a few side-roads of your own to explore while she is, as aforesaid, gathering flowers, so that she doesn't know *quite* what you're up to, it's an exercise for both of you.

Always keep something back.

If she's somewhat hazy about what your potentialities are she won't know quite where she has you. Territory fully explored tends to lose interest, and a bit of bafflement to the Opposition is always a handy weapon. So keep a small element of Mystery about you.

I don't necessarily imply that you should wear a Yashmak, though I have known cases where it would have been beneficial. But don't let her know all about you.

Keep one shot in the locker.

When the Child—writing you off as having one foot in the grave and being unworthy of consideration—deliberates as to whether she will go to Austria or Sweden this year for holidays or try the South Pole for a change—riposte smartly and with as bored a voice as you can muster—"Well, I do feel that Europe is a *wee* bit chewed-over. And the South Pole's *over-run* with helicopters and things. Personally I thought of going to Tahiti. And by cargo-boat. The planes are *so* noisy and drab!"

Her end of the see-saw will drop to earth with a mighty

wallop and yours will correspondingly soar. One's just *got* to keep one's end up sometimes.

Mind you—you'll have to be *prepared* to go to Tahiti after that if need be, (so you'd better get busy on a grass skirt. I have a nice pattern for crochetting one out of garden raffia) or to prison, or the moon, or Russia, or wherever you have rashly suggested.

You must never make either a boast, or a threat or a promise, that you are not prepared to implement if necessary. Though you

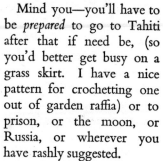

can always keep your fingers crossed and trust that your bluff will not be called.

But I do stress that you must Never Tell her All. Or if you do, then tell it slightly slantwise. Keep her guessing and she will hang back to investigate and explore. The result of her explorations will slow her down slightly and may well jolt her out of her complacency, as exemplified by the tail-end of a recent telephone conversation, accidentally overheard— "—and what do you *think* my dear! Just when we were ready to go, she came sweeping down, wearing one of those airy sort of white stole things that I've been trying to buy *everywhere* and couldn't find. The Old Devil had knitted it herself with baby wool and two wooden skewers and the stitch we used to make dish cloths with. And I didn't even know she could knit!"

Ignoring the blatant disrespect and the deplorable placing of the preposition, this wail-from-the-heart is a good symptom. It indicates that parental territory which Child has considered fully explored, is still capable of producing unsuspected features, and perhaps merits rather more than the perfunctory attention it would otherwise have received.

The country of the young is not necessarily an island inhabited by idiots and surrounded by archangels, but neither is the reverse the case.

As to moulding her a little nearer to your heart's desire— considered as virgin clay a daughter is some of the finest material in the world on which to work. But if one is to do anything with clay it must be kept soft and workable. Let it get a hard crust and it will need such knocking-about as will exhaust you before you've made any impression upon it.

And if you are to keep pace with her and get any good out of it she must be in a receptive and malleable state with no crust.

You think sometimes perhaps that she is lazy? And you're probably dead right.

One day she is a dynamo of enthusiasm and energy—full of bounce and bubbling over with good humour. The next finds her dull, morose, lethargic and utterly indifferent to every project you may care to put before her.

But don't either worry or fuss. This Stop-Go rhythm is typical of nature. Did you ever know a pear tree that fruited every year alike? And our natural span being less than that of trees our spasms of activity and laziness come closer together. It is merely a necessary recuperative process.

Inaction is not necessarily non-productive. Even in what is normally frowned upon as "day-dreaming" the dream may eventually be a reality. Indeed, the lazy teenager who is accused of wool-gathering may, after all, turn out to have been gathering the Golden Fleece and in her dreamy do-nothing-ness be accumulating some mental energy that will later surprise and confound her contemporary rushers-around.

But when you think the recuperation has gone far enough you might wisely decoy her into some activity by your own interest and sympathy.

She *is* interesting, especially if she is a so-called "Problem Child".

Since these invariably have infinitely more spirit, greater potentialities, and greater versatility than the "never a moment's trouble since she was born", or "suet pudding" type, thank your stars and watch your step. It's going to be fun all the way for you.

The young are shy birds.

Pursuit is fatal. But, if you can contrive to *entice* them with the right grain, they may in time come to eat out of your hand.

I don't know what your particular kind of bait may be—a little
gentle flattery—an absorption in
some ploy of your own which
may tempt her to try it—a sincere
sympathy, loyalty and dependa-
bleness—you must have got *something* that appeals to her if it's only
the art of letting her alone.

But not *too* much alone.

Why do you think she *bothers* to
be naughty? Why in order to be
noticed of course.

It seems only yesterday that we
sang at Children's Services "Can a
mother's tender care cease towards
the child she-bear?" Of course it
can but you would be well advised
not to let it do so and to be most
tender when she is most she-
bear-ish.

Stand by her, even if it develops
into a contest of You Two Against the World. It's *got* to
be, or you won't be able to rub the face of the Opposition
in the mud and prove that the bad ones are the best after
all.

She's only developing her spiritual muscles, much as a
baby cries to develop his lungs, kicks to develop his legs,
and a strong man poses to develop his ego. Be sympathetic to these exhibitions, or even welcome them as
a prelude to strength, but ignore them at your peril, for
the more she is ignored the more "enfant terrible" she will
be.

However when she realises that you were the same—that you spangled your youth and the youths of not a few others with actions varying from injudicious to rash and downright crazy and language which was as forceful—if not so varied—as her own, she will give up trying to create a sensation.

If it was done in *your* day, she will argue that it's outmoded now and has ceased to be either terrible or infantile.

But it's no use treating her like a bad smell and pretending that she's not there. Her attitude will be—"Well I'm damned! What haven't I got that the others have?" and the clamour for attention re-doubled until it reaches preposterous lengths. Draw her into what you can, *entice* her towards what you can't, so that she enters of her own accord and for heaven's sake don't be smug.

Mothers don't necessarily know *best*, only *more* and you may yet prove to be mistaken in many ways.

Agreed that she's a bombshell, a problem, a menace, a responsibility, she is also a delight, and treated as such—not as a juvenile delinquent—she will go quietly.

II

The Good Die Young

Give me a good digestion, Lord,
And also something to digest;
Give me a healthy body, Lord,
With sense to keep it at its best.
Give me a healthy mind, good Lord,
To keep the good and pure in sight
Which seeing sin is not appalled,
But finds a way to set it right.
Give me a mind that is not bored,
That does not whimper, whine or sigh,
Don't let me worry overmuch
About this fussy thing called "I".
Give me a sense of humour, Lord,
Give me the grace to see a joke,
To get some happiness in life
And pass it on to other folk.

Prayer in Chester Cathedral

THE chapter heading by no means implies undue mortality among those coyly referred to as "of tender years". The evidence is all against it.

Who's to decide how good is good anyway, or how many of them qualify for the title. And "tender" years is a hideous misnomer. They're about as tender as hoof-parings and as destructible as razor blades.

No, it merely indicates that youth is not an age, it is a state of mind—the state of being enthusiastic, unsatisfied, adventurous, careering from one discovery to another in a continuous headlong treasure-hunt, (though by no means always the same treasure) until one dies.

If you have an inquiring mind, a *relishing* kind of mind that likes to turn over strange tit-bits of queer flavour on the tongue, the little wheels of your invention will be set in motion by every new wind that blows. You can spin out your youth and enthusiasm for a whole life-time, although that is not enthusiasm's *reason*, only its result.

But unfortunately I can't tell you where to find these treasures, these titillating ideas and invigorating breezes.

They don't come entirely from books or from any of the arts, which would all be mute unless there existed some vibrating chord within yourself to which they could speak and have their voices heightened and given back again. It is a something within the human spirit which responds to an unpredictable stimulus, lights up, glows visibly and eventually pales again as you pass on to the next bit of treasure trove.

The only real essential is that you should always be reaching for *something*, preferably slightly beyond your grasp.

Never a dull moment. And you never know where you're going to trip over it.

By and large, a dahlia looks an unlikely object of affection, but I once knew a man with the urge to breed better and bigger dahlias (an attempt in which he was embarassingly successful). He kept himself busy hopping from show to show at a great rate all the autumn and pottering in the pottering shed or gardening with them in the garden at all other times of year.

At night when it was too dark to tell an earwig from a toad-in-the-hole he lost himself among the lying literature of catalogues, and the biggest and most technicoloured lies he believed most of all, which shows you to what a remarkable degree he had retained his youth.

He infinitely enjoyed brooding among the blowsy brutes and *doing nothing.*

But his wife *didn't enjoy doing anything* and there is a world of difference in the attitude to life.

She did her brooding indoors, adding up the hours during which he had preferred the dahlias to herself, even though she and they looked remarkably the same. And in the end when the hours had added up to days and years she turned sour, and had a screaming fit at breakfast over his interest in a new catalogue.

She returned, all glum, to her Mum, but her husband had custody of the children and now they all breed dahlias together, each as young and enthusiastic as the next and have even attained a quite unintentional fame and a good deal of money by it.

But that was as nothing compared with our village grocer, who decided, in his middle sixties, to study Arabic. Some stray thought gleaned from a date-box probably bit him where it was most deadly, so that when he might more reasonably have been engrossed entirely in grocering and stray thoughts about his imminent exit from this vale of tears, he took himself to night school twice a week as soon as the shutters were up and began to live all over again.

I will not exaggerate.

He never *did* manage to speak it.

Not so that he could understand what he was saying.

He knew what he meant, but the hiatus between the high planes of his thought and the gates of speech was never entirely bridged. However it didn't matter.

What *does* matter is not that you arrive, but that you travel hopefully and that you have pleasant and instructive adventures upon the road. The whole of that grocer's latter life (until he suddenly stopped living in mid-stride, at 83, and fell to sleeping from pleasant weariness) was one long picaresque novel.

He learned to read Arabic and unearthed such plums of philosophy, history and impropriety as kept him (though looked upon by his neighbours as a madman) chuckling and sane, when rationing would have driven a saner man mad.

He delved into Arabian geology, geography, biography, poetry, archaeology and mythology in such a way that he was never *finished* delving. There were always more treasures in the storehouse and life was all too short for the amount of excavating which was lying in an endless glorious vista all round him waiting to be done. And he had no time to be exasperated by the petty irritations of the nearer world.

They were just so many midges which he brushed aside when they bothered him.

You can imagine what a comfort he was to his family. The War was powerless to interrupt him and was kept firmly in its proper place. He was still deep in the strategy, stratagems, shifts, successes and subjugations of another war which raged around the years 634–644 A.D. but was still pretty lively reading exactly thirteen-hundred years later.

It gave him a sense of permanence and continuity, as if he had casually snared a slice of eternity and held it, like whiskered Stilton, within his hand. He felt that considering the way the ancients whammed at each other with no holds barred, and the little it had done to change the local scenery, he wasn't going to begin worrying now.

So every time a siren blew it was neither an irritation nor alarm, but a heaven-sent opportunity to stop grocering and whip out his homework, while the family, in order to keep pace with him, took up fretwork and crossstitch and stopped worrying too.

These two examples just happened to be male, but the exhibition of obstinate enthusiasm can be equally rooted in women.

Take my friend Annabelle for instance. At forty-five she was in a bad state, devoured and slain by dullness.

She couldn't bear to think about her Latter End and shuddered at the thought of her Former, whereas the Present was of no interest to her at all.

She spent her life in fleeing from them all (and being overtaken) and because every road, every diversion, was open to her, desired none of them, except as an escape from the others.

There was a daughter about the place somewhere though they rarely met, Annabelle being of the opinion that if you can afford to pay a governess to bark you'd be a fool to play watchdog yourself. Though she was perpetually oozing with grumbles and moans (or groans and mumbles) that she never *saw* the child; that everyone in the house went their own way and no-one cared a fig how Mamma fared.

I wouldn't know whether they were ever in step or not. They never got close enough to make any comparison.

But the girl being sane and normal and nineteen, occupied herself well with this and that, including her dog, Joey, a boxer (as if it mattered) who was of such difficult dimensions that he was too large to fit any ready-made kennel, too destructive to house within-doors and too precious to board with the vet.

Having considerable ingenuity and sundry male associates Jane (did I say that was her name?) purchased a collection of curious boards and bits labelled, "Do-it-yourself-henhouse. Keep them warm and they will lay" and the necessary metal objects with which to bang, pierce, cut or slice it into reasonable coherence. And in due course she spent many happy hours in what was called "The small East Room" (because they had already exhausted the better names of Dining, Music, Drawing, Billiard-room, Library, Boudoir and Den) making it cohere.

The fact that it was subsequently discovered to be immovable through either door or window, is not relevant and is nothing like so sad as the case of my cousin by marriage who built a boat in the drawing-room. But that's not relevant either.

What *is*, is that Annabelle, on a tour of more than usual boredom and despair, discovered the Kennel and, because it was something utterly outside her experience, it hit her slap amidships.

Picking up the chart and comparing it with its corporate realisation before her, it was obvious that the latter was unseaworthy (don't interrupt. I know kennels are not sailing craft but I've got to keep my vocabulary aired) and muttering "Clot! she's got that mortice on upside down" she seized a hammer and speedily put the matter right.

Humming now, with the years rolling off her like fur off an over-ripe rabbit, and all kinds of atavistic instincts—which merely means that her grandfather had been a builder—rushing to her aid, she made a really good job of the End Elevation and when the luncheon gong sounded was discovered with her face not yet done and not even having taken her reducing pills, happily measuring the dog to see if four-foot-six would go into three-foot-nine.

From that, progress to higher things was natural and inevitable.

She now spends all her time making delightful dwellings for the Displeased Persons who work on her country estate and her Will, both closely supervised by her daughter.

And when either of these objects is declared structurally unsound they scrap it and make another.

But they are together, synchronised and bashing about in unison.

Annabelle not only derives the keenest delight and considerable merriment from the thought of what will happen when her final Will is read, she is making full use of the past and cramming the present so full that it's running over at the edges.

Young? She's practically infantile and it's all her Daughter can do to control her.

As for myself; it was the Oboe. Having heard one, bought one, studied its construction, mechanism, history and biography there remains nothing now but to play it.

This I have never, so far, accomplished. But that is not to say that I never *will*. To keep on trying is an exercise in enthusiasm and aspiration. Particularly aspiration. And the muscle exercises are good for the face.

Moreover (possibly in order to beat me on my home ground) the Girl-child has achieved considerable proficiency on the recorder, flute and skiffle whistle. As usual we are in it together—with both feet—and still nicely keeping step.

And if anyone cares to compose a concerto for curtain-pole and oboe (mute) we shall be pleased to consider its production.

III

Safe Conduct for Mothers

I BELIEVE it's an axiom that you can't have too much of a good thing. Therefore you'd better make your first tottering and hazardous steps in this pace-keeping game right at the start. Because from the moment she's born she'll have the tendency to elude you. You can see the superior thoughts whiffling over her sleeping face, like wind blowing over wheat, before she's six months old, and to fling any poor woman into such a hazardous occupation as Daughter-rearing without long and arduous training is an act of unparalleled callousness.

To the mother, naturally.

The child will come out of it all right, but to the harassed parent, handling material with such a low flash point and high explosive capacity as a daughter—*any* daughter—the way is scarred with bombholes and blasts.

Some International Committee should set up a Mother Guidance Bureau with classes, diplomas and charts of the track. Otherwise you will take a detour round one danger-point, jump a second and land flat on your face in a third before you know it's there. It's too late to put up the caution signals when you're dusting yourself down from one encounter and preparing to step backwards into the next.

But, as is well known, people who fall softest and with least hurt are drunken men and imbeciles, owing to their relaxed nature. So if not naturally belonging to these two privileged classes you'd better begin early, get alongside this strange new being in her cradle and take your time from *her*, instead of trying to force her into *your* mould. You should then automatically make an even progress together without strain or haste on either side.

No mother will quarrel with this. The one absolute essential for a child's mental health is a warm, placid, and personal relationship with her female parent and it's equally beneficial to the mother.

Child feels the warm glow of pride and interest from her mother—mother receives it back from the confidence and dependence of the child and it does something for both of them which they can't get in any other way.

It isn't anything you can learn from books or plan on paper, it comes from the inner needs of both of you, which can only be satisfied and completed by the other. Just as food is not a question of proteins, carbohydrates and fat alone—as earth is not merely nitrogen, phosphates and potash—so child-and-mother welfare is not so many hours each of sleep—exercise —eating and nothing more. There is an elusive element in each—food, earth, motherhood—that defies precise analysis but transmutes them from the mechanical to the real and provides them with a soul.

That being so, and I believe the evidence is overwhelming that it *is* so, you can see that from the earliest moment, if we attack the job properly and scientifically, we are keeping pace with our young and getting a terrific kick out of it.

Lacking, as we unfortunately do, any Guide Book for Lost Mothers the pace is likely at times to be slightly syncopated. There will be a permanent Stop-Go quality about your progress as you alternately lag behind or over-run her, and every now and then there will be a dense fog and entire absence of signals so that you don't even know where she is. Much less the location of your own whereabouts.

You have slightly less idea what is going on in her mind than before she could talk. In fact it was of her that the philosopher declared "Speech is given to us to conceal our thoughts with", and recklessly concluded his sentence with a preposition.

She chats in a superficial way with her friends and with you, but you know that it is the crackling of thorns under a pot—even the occasional sound and fury signify nothing. She is quite inaccessible; apparently unemotional; neither offers nor demands anything from anyone, least of all yourself, until suddenly you realise that the whole thing is a gigantic act. She's preoccupied with the early stages of living and can best do it by herself, therefore your wisest course is not to interrupt.

Don't expect too much too soon.

And if it isn't what you expect when it comes, don't complain.

Never make a major issue of anything or take a stand on some relatively unimportant matter. It could be difficult to retreat afterwards, but if you let byegones be byegones, harbour no grudges and preach no sermons (though you can practise them if it makes you feel any better) the way is always open for discussion and negotiation when required.

You are not a policeman, but a companion. It's the only capacity in which you'll ever keep beside her. And if by any chance you'd thought of putting on a strong act as a Saint or a Martyr or a Sorrowing Mother let me at once restrain you. The young have a sure instinct for the bogus and if you try any meretricious nonsense of this kind she'll smell it out and from ignoring you as an equal, grow to despise you as a humbug. And serve you right.

You can't even use your age (even if you admit it) and your parental authority (if it exists) to enforce some argument which is fundamentally unsound or illogical. It's a confession of weakness.

Can't you see that Age is not a certificate of merit? It's not even an asset. Only an accident, and no guarantee of wisdom unless you've used the years carefully and painfully in acquiring it.

To drag up your heavy artillery and introduce the fortuitous circumstance of age into a discussion which could better be settled man to man, as contemporaries and reasonable human beings, is to leave the affair inconclusive and honour unsatisfied. In fact it's as mean a refuge as going into a bare-fist fight wearing knuckle dusters, and I hope you lose.

In any case you're throwing away the thing we're trying like mad to acquire. The illusion of youth in our middle-aged desert. The feeling and appearance of contemporaries rather than parents. You can't have it both ways, saying "I know best because I'm older" and at the same time demanding to walk with her as her equal and her friend.

No, it's no use. We'd better crawl down from our chilly eminence, throw away our halo and the mantle of omniscience and hope the children didn't see us in our "heavy parent" role.

They very likely know best after all. Though *how* they acquire the knowledge beats me to discover. Perhaps all children are born knowing everything and they haven't yet had time to forget it.

You send her to school. Alas you are *obliged* to perform this callous gesture and spend the next ten years with a split personality, suffering not only your own hurts but hers as well. And what happens?

Shielded by her personality from the hazards and horrors of education she emerges apparently unscathed by any taint of scholarship, unmarked by any association, retaining only a series of negative impressions. She dislikes school-meals/games/beds/marms/prefects, but otherwise she is still a blank waiting to receive some distinctive mould.

You send her hopefully, and at enormous cost, to Switzerland and await the emergence of her pattern, polished and perfected into something charming and mature.

I don't have to tell you *again* do I? You *know*!

She has a more comprehensive set of dislikes now—corridors—fir trees—parquet—Swiss plumbing—embryo Debs—cowbells—mountains—French—snow and all snowy sports. She is proficient only in bridge and swearing (in four languages) and devoted only to the memory of one ski-instructor, one dog and one village postman's son who, bearing his ski-broken neck jauntily in a plastic dish upon his shoulders, has the aura of a stricken hero as well as undeniable good looks.

You might think this a poor halfpennyworth of return for the monstrous great deal of outlay that went into it, And if you do, then I say that it's a mercenary and unworthy thought.

This was not a banking transaction in which you sink four-pence in order that in due course it may be returned to you as sixpence. Shame on you.

And why worry anyway?

A little probing discovers that she has educated herself in her absence, in all that matters. Education is well known to come in two brands—the kind you *get* to live, and the kind you *live* to get, and it's a good dose of the latter to which she's been helping herself, all unobserved.

She is now logical, reasonable, discriminating. Her vision is keen and her values true—truer than those of her parents, who have imbibed so many of other folk's ideas that they are now no longer sure what *they* think and what other people have thought *for* them. Their whole outlook is muzzy round the edges and slightly soiled.

No-one is infallible, not even the youngest among us—but she is at least looking at life with new eyes from a new angle, and is more probably right than we are, who survey it backwards and upside-down.

Her roots go down to the depths of the world; she absorbs wisdom from the earth she treads and from every hour's existence on it. She is your darling and your divining rod, and in the up-welling springs of her pure wisdom and pristine logic you may refresh and renew yourself by her side.

If you take careful heed and imbibe respectfully such wisdom as she cares to impart, you will be taking your education together and should become extremely friendly in the course of that enjoyable process.

It's much more reasonable and beneficial that we should adapt ourselves to the young than they to us. Put some thought into it and a bit of sense; patch up the holes in yourself that she has already discovered, then go round to her side of the counter and take a really good look at yourself from her point of view.

Few mothers are complete write-offs. Though some are more written-off than others. But in all of us there is something on which the young can build. Some feature, characteristic, attribute or accomplishment, from which, if we listen carefully to her pronouncements, we can produce a newer, more attractive mother.

Moreover, realizing that she is educating Mamma, she will be careful to teach, both by precept and example, nothing but what is good and becoming.

The young are very conscious of the appearance and conduct of their parents and if these latter paid more attention to the children's advice they wouldn't look (or be) so peculiar.

In addition to this great boon the pace of the children will be modified to that of the aged, tottering parents whom they guide.

No shepherd rushes on ahead of his sheep.

This ensures a sweet unity and a family progress resembling rather a minuet than a tarantella. And if at times the pair of you appear to be leaping and bucking like a brace of trout, it's all part of the dance and very enlivening for the beholders.

IV

Conversation Piece

BEFORE you can keep pace with *anyone* you've got to get acquainted with them. Strange and unwelcome events befall those who walk and talk with Strangers. But if she is strange it's your own fault.

She is your child, not merely an announcement in *The Times* on a certain date half your lifetime away. She is your other self, with your own blood, and therefore approach and intimacy should be easy. But let it be on *her* plane. It is for *you* to go to *her* not expect her, yet, to come to you. That will follow later.

The past is alien territory to the Young. A foreign soil in which trees bear strange fruit, wild beasts lurk and the uncouth fore-runners of today's familiar friends boast two faces.

Naturally it is territory utterly without charm for them, dismissed with a shudder of distaste and an elevation of the nose, indicating that things are now better done than in those dismal days.

You can't expect the young to be much interested in what happened when you were their age. There is no parallel and it is useless and presumptuous to wring a sermon out of it. Moreover, the morals you draw will produce in her more gooseflesh than confidence.

Their ancestors—meaning You and Me—muddled through somehow in the dim light of their primordial ignorance, but, lacking all the attributes of civilisation, one couldn't expect them to be very bright. And the children are usually (and courteously) prepared to make allowances.

This is your cue and you've got to play it that way or not at all. Allow them to explain Life to you, with or without a capital. Rely on their wisdom to modernise you, so that you can shake off the cobwebs and emerge into their daylight, the harsh and ruthless present, and perhaps even be a credit to them. It's the only common ground you are likely to find, so you'd better take an interest in what's going on, who is at the moment Who, what is What (though this is liable to vary daily), and the current list of Those with Whom one wouldn't be seen dead.

Discuss all things with her—if she wishes to discuss them—but remember that discussions are not unilateral. A good listener is at least as valuable in every conversation as a good talker and infinitely more so in discussions with the young.

We can't all run races. *Someone* has to stand by the track and cheer, and you'd better resign yourself to the role of cheer-leader until she has run this particular race, handicapped as she is by her very youth, enthusiasm and inexperience, and brought it to a triumphant conclusion.

You are still with her, even when you're only standing-by. So cultivate the art of listening to her. Sit quietly and let her talk, no matter if it is two in the morning and you are dropping with fatigue and she is sitting on the end of your bed chirruping cheerfully about some apparently irrelevant matter. She is talking, but with no sense of destination in her talk. Nor time either. Just round and round, to eternity and back.

Don't be in a hurry. Don't interrupt. Don't argue.

And don't complain about her language, it's a sign that all her guards are down and she's meeting you as man to man.

Above all don't let your eyes close, even if you have to pinch yourself under the bedclothes to keep awake.

Let her chirrup, and eventually the kernel of the conversation towards which she has been imperceptibly heading for the last hour, will emerge.

You are a highly privileged woman and it's worth the loss of a little sleep. You'd lose a lot more if she *didn't* confide in you, so what are you grumbling at?

When I lived in Ireland there was a saying that "there are three fewnesses that are better than plenty: a fewness of fine words; a fewness of cows on grass; a fewness of good friends round old ale", and it's the first of these that you must now exhibit.

You'll never know what's going on inside her (infinitely more important than what goes on *outside*) and never get to grips with the real "her" at all if you don't train yourself to listen, not only to what she *says*, but to the tone in which she says it and even the hesitance and intervals between the words.

But *listen* and don't fidget, with your ear turned to her and your mind in the oven.

I don't care if you *are* worried about what's happening to the pastry.

Blow the pastry!

Or throw it away or give it to the dog. Do anything you like to it. Give it to the birds and live on love!

Don't you realise, lady, that this is a highly critical period of your life? *Both* your lives? You are her guide, philosopher and friend and if you take a pride in your job you've got to listen, not only to the words but to the inflexion. And not least, to the things she doesn't say. Give not only your ear but your heart. To apply the appropriate treatment for her troubles (which may be merely to remain diplomatically mute) you have to use your imagination and understanding —not only laugh or cry, but to do it at the *right moment*.

And here let me wag a sharp admonitory finger at Mums who, having received Daughters' confidence and confidences retail them under a pledge of strictest secrecy to their friends.

It is a piece of base disloyalty—a dreadful sin and a selling of one of your most priceless possessions for a moment's chit chat over the teacups. Moreover it is usually (unless she is a garbage sifter of the first degree) embarrassing to the recipient. If the child walks in on you during one of these indiscreet revelations the deadly hush, or interpolation of some hurried

red herring, will Tell Her All, and you will be properly up the creek. And serve you right.

Your punishment will fit the crime.

You can't be *executed* for it, but she will never trust you again, and that hurts more and longer.

Moreover, having spent years building up her sense of safety and security, you have demolished the whole show with some careless word of tittle-tattle, which leaves her in mid-air, unsupported, and with her faith in the whole universe undermined.

Even if she doesn't discover you "in flagrante delicto", the betrayed confidence will probably leak round, as these things unexplicably *do*.

Of course you made the stipulation to your friend, "But don't say a word". So did *she* when she retailed it, and the next one too. It's a form of crossing the fingers, but it never works and a betrayal is treachery whether you've sold a pass or only a child. So watch your step. Mum's the world.

However, to get back to the Daughter. For the proper production of confidences, I think some mutual occupation is a powerful aid. Words come easier if you can fiddle with something while you talk.

Perhaps you could learn to *make* something together, whether it's jam, jig-saws, alms bags, almond macaroons, hay, haggis, models or only mistakes.

Or not even *making*, perhaps just *studying* something, like footmarks on the tennis-lawn after snow (by which you can demonstrably prove to all and sundry that overnight you have been visited by two ducks, a prevalence of partridges, a pride of tom-cats, a two-toed sloth and an Abominable Snowman), or the singularly economical habits of the caddis-worm.

But whatever it is, do it together, so that ideas get into the habit of flowing from one open mind to the other, with neither of you bothering to translate them, to sift your facts, or save your face, but all free and uninhibited, with no dark spots marked "Danger, keep out".

And, mark you, when I say unin*hib*ited I don't mean unin*hab*ited. You don't need to be witless in order to be amiable and if each side has its opinions about the subject in hand—can justify them by logical reasoning and exchange them amicably with the sane and certain knowledge that an argument is not necessarily either a quarrel or an exercise in brute force, your joint creation, whatever it may be, will be a better and a sounder job.

But its best effect, like most of life's valuable productions, will be invisible. It will get you both into the habit of working and talking together, swapping notions and emotions unselfconsciously, with all the guards down and a blessed feeling of unity and peaceful comprehension between you—a Freemasonry of two.

In cold blood, without the bond of mutual employment she is likely to remain aloof, disdainful and secretive, shut firmly into her cocoon of cotton wool. The very best cotton wool no doubt, but a bad bit of bafflement for anyone who wants to get through it and have a look at the Daughter inside.

It really doesn't matter *what* you do. Feeling, touching, seeing, hearing are all natural channels of expression, aids to fuller living and mutual comprehension.

Even at home you can study an infinite variety of things—how to receive graciously some unwanted guest, compliment, gift or invitation—to be impervious to annoyance or accident—to be impartial to friends or enemies and above all how to avoid boredom by centring one's every thought and interest on the potential borer.

But the finest get-together aid is some new subject, and the further out of your joint grasp the better. The effort to master it will keep you leaping and be more beneficial than much learning (which is an arid, sterile possession). It's not necessarily any achievement I'm after, it's the joint endeavour which counts.

Meet on equal terms, or rather better than equal so far as she is concerned. And it is advisable for your mutual good that you should not beat her either at work or play. But don't worry. You won't in any case.

There is nothing more endearing to the young than a parent on whom they can shower good-natured scorn. One who is less successful than themselves at some minor art or craft, one whom they may instruct and assist to higher things with lofty condescension.

Conversely, there is no parent who is less popular than he (or even more so *she*) who is efficient at all things and knows it.

She is a blight and a pain in the neck and will be very properly left to endure her chilly perfection alone.

So if you can tackle your mental or manipulative limbering-up exercises together and let it gradually dawn on her that she's better at it than you, so much the better for your mutual relationship.

You make mistakes together but *you* make the most. You possibly finish together, but her finish has more finish than yours. You are trying hard but you don't *quite* bring it off. And you needn't be an *utter* fool either (unless you were *born* that way) but just slightly off the beam.

In no time at all she will be adapting her pace to yours, realising that you are a mere infant in the higher reaches where she soars, and her own pride and confidence will drive her to surprising heights if she really thinks she's *getting* somewhere.

Naturally, if you ever let it slip that the Academy took a little thing of yours in 1934—or that you have a gold medal for bee-hiving knocking about among your hairgrips—or sang solos in a cathedral and can accompany concert singers in the dark—it's your own silly fault if she immediately ceases to be sympathetic and charming.

I have no patience with you.

It's *her* turn for the limelight now. She's got to have some *real* basis for the attention of the crowd or she will perpetuate some brassy and injudicious audacity to attract it. It's stupid of you to blow the dust off your own decently interred laurels and bring them out to deck your brow again, all rakish and demodé and brown round the edges as they are, and leave her, resentful, in the rear.

You had your day and now you are having your second chance—living vicariously in unison and sympathy with her and feeling every heart-beat of it, good or bad. What more do you want?

If she's half the girl I think she is, after a short course of Instruction to Mothers, her apprehensions and timidities—the twin locks on adolescent speech—will be lulled to sleep and you will enter each other's minds freely without knocking, wandering the delightful territory and treading the same paths at will.

You won't even *know* you are keeping pace with her, because it will be effortless and unconscious—speech untranslated and unbowdlerised—thoughts on plain view—cupboards unlocked and not a skeleton in sight—the most delightful companionship in the world. But it's up to you to ensure it.

You'd better get into practice right away.

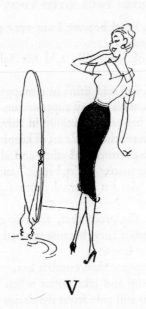

V

Keeping Up Appearances

Tʜᴇʀᴇ is no doubt that if you wish to keep within hailing
distance of your daughter or even within several streets
of her you've got to preserve a good appearance.

Not only a *good* one but a *suitable* one which again is
something different.

"Ethel Monticue," we are told at the outset of her meteoric
career, " had fair hair done on the top and blue eyes. She had
a blue velvit frock which had grown rarther short in the
sleeves. She had a black straw hat and kid gloves."

So we can see that she was really trying.

When the Great Day arrived and the Young Visiter was
about to set forth on her travels: "I shall put some red ruge

on my face said Ethel because I am very pale owing to the drains in this house

"You will look very silly said Mr Salteena with a dry laugh.

"Well so will you said Ethel in a snappy tone and she ran out of the room with a very superier run throwing out her legs behind and her arms swinging in rithum"

And there we have the whole art of keeping up appearances, dress, hair-do, deportment, rhythm and all—with a fine bit of bravado in the matter of "red ruge," and a sensible adherence to her theories on external decoration with the devil taking the critics.

There is even the proof that, according to the standards of her day, she was a lady, because she had put on her gloves before leaving the house.

We might do worse than emulate her.

Do people sit up and take notice when you sweep into a room, or are you still pale from the drains or something?

Is there a rhythm between the way you swing your arms and throw your legs out behind? If not perhaps your callisthenics need some attention.

Do you match your frock with your eyes?

Admittedly if you have the odd sort, one blue, one brown it might be just a mite awkward, otherwise go to it, lady, the effect can be stunning.

And you notice that "her blue velvit frock had grown rarther short in the sleeves". Pure feminine humbug. It wasn't her *arms* that had grown too *long*? Oh no, the sleeves had somehow dwindled and she had the art to leave it at that and probably even to push them up a bit further, to convince all beholders that they were *meant* to look that way.

It's an art, that's what it is, like wearing an old rag so that it looks like mink or mink so that it looks like old rag and anything in between so that it looks as if you hadn't given a thought to whether it's mink *or* rag.

If you have a defect, probably one which your daughter has kindly revealed to you, play it up, dear, don't play it *down*. "How to disguise a high brow" say the hairdressing magazines. "How to disguise your broad cheek bones/snub nose/one-sided smile"—or whatever you have.

Why at one time they even counselled you to darken your white forelock! Now white forelocks are being mass-produced by the million. My advice to you is to keep it, whatever you have. It's the only thing in the world that is truly yours and likely to be the only thing by which you will be remembered.

If your brow is high then *raise* it, even if you look like a Chinese. Play up your cheek bones, high-light your retroussé nose, and lipstick your crooked smile until it looks like an appendicitis scar slipped sideways. Sooner or later someone is sure to say that you look like Mona Lisa and that's fame and reward enough for you.

But if you're going to hold your own in this race for glamour and have enough of what it takes to stand beside your own daughter, you've got to have a line of your own. Forget about giving yourself a New Look, just develop the one you've got. It will take less holding and you'll have more time to manage it to advantage. It will be at least an original work of art.

I remember that a few years ago there was a record crop of Elizabeth Taylors. The world was over-run with raven-haired, sooty-eyebrowed, pneumatic charmers, their eyelids apparently hung with black lamp-fringe, all utterly indistinguishable one from the other.

The next year M. Dior decreed that busts were no longer beautiful and they deflated in a flash, as flat as flounders.

A subsequent wind, blowing from another quarter, turned hair blonde and Eton cropped, emulating the young lady in certain milk advertisements and now they are all gamine Audrey Hepburns, hounded into anonymity by their immoderate devotion to yet another ideal.

But we are too old to follow the herd.

If you take your Personality to a party you want to play it. What's the use of herding by the wall with a dozen other undistinguished matrons, slyly eyeing the Woman Who is Being Looked At, to see what she's got that we haven't?

We would rather be The Woman.

I prefer to make my own Impact rather than envy the Impacts of others. Go get me a gimmick and we will begin.

There's no reason at all why at forty (well slightly more if you like, but I'm being generous) you should sink into sloth, despondency, WX and good works, when you might be carving out a distinguished niche for yourself and hitting such high spots as are available. It's just a question of courage and building up on what you've got. Building up on a good foundation in fact, whether it's your bones, your belt, your bra or your beauty cream. But have a heart lady! Don't overdo it. Because I say you are not done for at *forty* it doesn't mean that you can get yourself up like *twenty* and simper coyly round the fringes of the fray like Leda looking for the Swan.

Let fitness in all things be our watchword.

We will discuss some comely ensembles.

If your hair has gone from gold to mouse and is now taking a downward plunge towards chinchilla, play it up. What have I already told you?

It's grey and you know it, and moreover your eyes have gone from the blue of Mediterranean seas to the blue of English ditto, which will do us nicely for a trimming. Clothe yourself in grey to match your hair, neat good suits with shirt blouses or woollies to match your eyes and plain frocks with clean lines. Eye-blue linen and nylon for summer will do you splendidly; grey or blue jersey for winter, and for formal evenings grey velvet, jersey, silver brocade or something delightfully chiffony in dusty pink. You could be as pretty as a picture.

With grey frocks or suits you can alternate the touches of blue with lime (black accessories) using rosy lipstick with the faintest hint of cyclamen and a clear but not clamorous powder.

For a change have a blue rinse to your hair (but not *too* blue), wear air-force-blue tweeds or frocks, with dull tan as the second colour and delicate grey accessories. The lipstick will have to be quieter and less blue than formerly and the powder more suntanned.

Jade green will suit you, with the major contrast in clear pale grey and accessories in "antelope" but you need a clear bright lipstick with this if the effect is not to be dingy and a rachel powder not too "foncée".

But for heaven's sake don't wear beige, camel, or sage. You'll look a mouse and a mess and no-one will be quicker to spot it than The Child. It is she to whom I have always, as now, flown for advice.

If you ask your husband he either doesn't *notice* or doesn't *know* or doesn't *care* and in any case will take the line of least resistance. If you ask your dressmaker she probably daren't tell you the truth. And if you are one of the lucky ones who can buy "off the peg", *they've* got to sell frocks, haven't they, and *you* want to buy one and the sooner the twain meet (be the result what it may) the better the vendeuse will be pleased and the quicker she can get to another customer, to turn on the sales talk all over again.

No, your Daughter is the one unbiased judge. She is born with a naturally sound critical sense and has been (we hope) allowed to exercise and develop it, learning by her mistakes while still caring passionately for her appearance—and yours if you are to be a credit to her.

Left to myself I would fish out the basic Little Black Frock from my wardrobe (the base of that collection for many years) and with a brief glance at any old "glossy" take what current advice they offered.

"Straight lines, no belt", that's all right. If I wear it back to front and stand with my back to the wall the lines are dead straight. And I've lost the belt anyway so that's O.K. too. "Warm it up with a touch of French mustard and lightly brown under the grill——" No, forget that one, I'd turned over two pages! But you see what mothers are. Better pass the responsibility to The Child.

Bless my soul, she knows the whole thing backwards and has studied it intently in every available magazine for years, whereas you can hardly tell a pleat from a peplum. Let her advise you and she won't *dare* to be wrong.

Let us have more advice from the same quarter.

For brown eyes and hair, brown frocks relieved with lime, chestnut accessories and clear red lipstick. Stick to any shade of brown for everything and you can add tangerine, nigger and camel to it as required. If you choose a sober nigger for the main item you may even, greatly daring, have peacock blue to lift it (and you) out of the rut, and a dash of wild rose pink somewhere. Sounds "a bit hijus", as she once remarked, but you can get away with it if you're *neat*.

The chestnut haired (whether the genuine article or acquired) can, contrary to belief, get away with anything, even purple and pink. They are well able to look after themselves and have the kind of temperament that doesn't mind if it *is* creating a sensation. With their beautiful skin and tawny eyes they don't have to worry.

But in each and every case it's no use choosing some arbitrary colour scheme, regardless of your natural assets. Find out what your theme song is and plug it. But whatever your assets I implore you, keep off those large and artistic patterns which are only fit for upholstery. You will *look* upholstered. Stick to small designs or none.

Don't wear full and bunchy skirts. They are for Daughters, not Mums.

If you have better ankles than your child, which is so often the case, see that your skirts emphasise them. Shorten them, spend a lot on your shoes, and see that your bag and gloves match them.

You can keep up a very distinguished appearance if you just

D

watch these few points and, as I said in the beginning, build up on a good and relatively costly foundation. It pays handsomely in the end.

There's no need to regret the years that have gone. Anywhere between forty and sixty you are just in the prime of life and can be equally as chic as The Child now you know how.

We may as well take leave of Ethel, going up "to change her wedding garment for a choice pink velvet frock with a golden gurdle and a very chick tocque" as she departed "for a merry six weeks of bliss in Egypt".

Girl has got Man, entirely, if you ask me, because she knew what her line was and clove to it. From velvet to velvet in one act so to speak.

So make yourself over into a New Mamma merely by picking the best bits out of the old one and no slacking. If you want to keep within step you've got to be as interested and intelligent and ingenious, in the matter of lipsticks and colour schemes and other Aids to Beauty, as the Child.

The thought of growing old—or, rather, of *not* growing old, but of being obliged to remain young—is admittedly somewhat depressing. But it becomes progressively *less* so, the more interest and enthusiasm we put into the process.

And if your technique is slightly shaky on any point take my tip and ask her advice. She will, I am sure, be only too happy to give it.

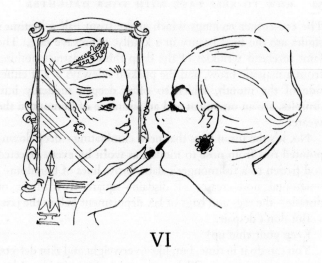

VI

Putting the Best Face On It

"Glamour glows in the face but is distilled in the stomach"
Me.

NOT THAT I am in favour of anything elaborate in the line of face-making. You can so easily over-do it, and a little over-enthusiasm can create a macabre ensemble of girlish giggles, dead-pan maquillage, and fluorescent hair with ineradicable wrinkles twittering uneasily beneath.

But if we keep our sense of proportion and know our limitations there's no harm in a spot of rejuvenation.

Actually I've nothing against wrinkles.

An unlined face is an unwritten page, and if no-one has written anything on you by the time you're forty there must be some sound reason for the neglect. If they're in the right place lines are merely a stressing point of pleasant character.

51

The eye-corner etchings which arrive from half a lifetime's smiles are the final beauty in a kindly, expressive face. The faint forehead wrinkles of the deep thinker detract nothing from a majestic brow, and the puckish sideways >'s at either side of the mouth, which so often deepen suddenly into dimples, are an ornament and an assurance of humour in the wearer.

No, it's the mean lines that need eliminating—deep down-pointed ruts from nose to mouth, as worn by every dejected cod frozen to a fishmonger's slab—brow lines of boredom—horizontal nose-creases of disdain—square frown-lines of distaste—the sags and bags of lax deportment below the jaw.

But don't despair.

Keep your chin up!

You can do it in time, but, like overweight and skin defects, any permanent cure will have to come from inside. It's a change of temperament you want lady.

For instance one of the best cures for the "cod" expression is whistling. But if you can whistle—laugh at yourself doing it, and then sing the Siamese National Anthem (O wa ta na Siam, which goes to the same tune as our own) out of the bottom corner of your mouth to complete the musical entertainment, you've got a cure for almost anything.

Try it and see:

Purse the lips and push them out as far as they will go, my pretty little rosebud.

Now grin with the widest and "cheesiest" laugh you can muster.

Finally twist your lower lip first to one side then to the other, with the upper one rigid, like a low comedian talking sotto-voce, and sing through the aperture.

Go on. Do it before a mirror.

You can't *help* seeing what a silly you look and the real, genuine laugh that follows is the best part of the treatment, because it's coming from the belly not the beauty parlour.

Of course, if you can't laugh at yourself you're a gone coon, a dead duck and a total loss to any theory. I can't help you and you can't even help yourself.

But if your temperament is of this very mature kind I'm afraid that you won't be able to keep pace with your daughter anyway.

You're gone too far.

However, you may still attack your facial shortcomings without effort by visiting a clinic. I know of one which practically makes you over like new in a dozen doses—massage, red veins, unwanted pleats, pimples, blotches, scars, bumps, spots—the lot—for a very moderate fee and it makes a nice rest while it's going on.

If you are one of those who think that people come only in three kinds, millionaires, rich millionaires and *very* rich millionaires, I can tell you of a place which alters you so much that in three weeks you wouldn't know yourself.

This is frequently a good idea.

I can recommend it if you are in a bored state/hurry/hiding/despair about your torso, features or effect on beholders.

There's really nothing they can't do. You just agree to the blueprint and they do the rest. When you first meet a long mirror at the end of a corridor you (*a*) think "Who is this elegant stranger who has crept among us?" and (*b*) try to walk past yourself, getting in a tizzy about the ensuing contradance and then banging your nice new nose.

But, as I said, it costs plenty and it's more fun to buy a do-it-yourself kit and undertake the rebuilding at home.

And in all cases you'd better consult the Young Woman

first. She might not like a complete stranger for a mother and you'd be further away from her than ever.

If you do it at home you'd better start from the bottom by attacking the basic causes and work upwards to results.

Why isn't your skin clear? And at the same time why is it always shiny? Eat more fruit and green vegetables, salads, orange juice and light food generally. Cut out fat, fried foods, pastry and alcohol and drink plenty of water, at least four glasses a day. In fact go on my reducing diet in the next chapter.

In a month you'll have a skin one can *see* through.

On the other hand if the skin is dry and rough take plenty of butter, cheese, and milk, in addition to the diet just mentioned and it will become soft and elastic.

You'd better knock off soap on the face too and use only a non-astringent cleansing cream.

Never mind what film stars are alleged to say about lathering themselves with "Frix" or "Frivol". They can *eat* it so far as I am concerned. Have you ever *seen* one? Really close up I mean. Then be warned and stick to rain water and cleansing cream. And if it doesn't rain in your part of the world buy a small water softener to stand beside your water supply and employ the result exclusively inside and out.

Have you ever given sulphur to the dog when its pelt was off-colour? Then take notice of the improvement. But you needn't take it neat. Onions, radishes, sprouts, eggs, cauliflower, cabbage, tomatoes, asparagus, horseradish, are all bursting with sulphur, but liable to lose it in cooking, so eat what you can of them raw.

A dry skin is usually fine and delicate but resents any form of alkali, which is one of the basic components both of soap and of hard water. Use also Milk of Roses foundation cream and a rich skinfood at night.

The chances are that your hand skin, also, is too dry, and if you're to look at all glamorous, or even presentable, we'll have to cure that at once. Remember we are trying to catch up with The Child who still has a pelt with all the elasticity of youth. We have to restore our lost texture in order to stand beside her and feel no shame. And you can do it!

Wear gloves whenever you can for gardening or household jobs. If that's too tedious use a "barrier cream" which seals the pores for about three hours. Always rub in a heavy hand-cream (the best one smells of laurel-leaves and is not greasy) after washing your hands, and use as little soap as possible.

Do ladle some cream on them at night too and wear a loose old pair of cotton gloves with the finger tips cut off for ventilation.

I *know* you'll feel like a muffled cat, but I know also that it's the only way to turn rough or wind-reddened or age-abused hands into a pair of magnolia petals. Truly! Though I'm too modest to tell you *how* I know.

So what's next?

There's a silly phrase stating that beauty lies in the eye of the beholder. A chancy business I *must* say. And how are you going to know what state the beholder's eye is in, and therefore how beautiful you look?

Sometimes you *can* tell, but these people are not considered nice for mothers to know, and before you can get down to details either he or you is/are removed.

No. It's nothing to do with beholders. Not yet. If it didn't sound so vulgar, or if I were less nice about words, I would tell you quite crudely that beauty comes from the stomach. Most of it. What you can't conjure up from inside you can admittedly plaster on from outside, but we've got to get you reformed from top to toe somehow and it's no use saying that the time is past when looks mattered to you. It's never past, and is more vital now, when you can't afford to let The Child get too far ahead of you, than ever. You are not yet part of the scenery, a mere background for her, so come out of it and get busy.

Hair now. Can you conscientiously describe it as your crowning glory? Or does it more resemble sofa stuffing or a lightly-fried loofah?

It's the old "inside-out" acus miracus or hocus-pocus. Do you get enough vitamins in your food? Enough sleep? Enough hatless exercise? And does your scalp get enough exercise too?

No dear, I don't mean scratching your head over the household accounts.

Brush with a stiff-bristled brush for five minutes by the clock every morning, brushing *towards the crown* and against the growth all round and finishing up with your head hanging down. Five minutes can seem a long time, but your scalp will tingle and glow and the hair become possessed by a life of its own, shiny, electric, and in time, if it is the right kind, developing the natural wave that has been killed by the permanent one.

You may fear that all this robust treatment will brush out your permanent. I doubt it, it's more likely to preserve it. But in any case better have a shine and no "perm" than the reverse. Anyhow perms are going out fast, and the careless, youthful, exuberant look of a shining, healthy head is a greater asset and less responsibility than the careful, matronly, slightly dried-out waves you bore formerly, as formal as the plumes of a funeral horse and as ageing as a birth certificate.

If your hair is dry don't wash it more often than once a fortnight. Use an egg shampoo or two egg yolks, rinse with beer, and dry as slowly as you can. A drier is murder to already dry hair. Get The Child to massage it for you with

Silvikrin hair tonic or "Petrole Hahn". Actually you could massage with almost anything from cocoa to cognac I believe, it's the massage that does the trick, and the diet régime is the same as for dry skin.

Greasy hair. I apologise for touching on these unpleasant topics, but if no-one else will tell you, and you don't want to look like Medusa, the Queen Gorgon, then *I* must.

Wash it once a week to get rid of the excess of grease, using a little dissolved boracic acid in the water. Go hatless whenever possible, and use a drying fluid (such as some spirit hair lotion) on the scalp every night.

You can do your hair, any old sort of hair, a power of good by eating the stuff that makes it grow—sulphur, iodine and silicone, and that even applies to grey hair, which will regain quite a lot of its colour under a proper régime of these foods, allied to massage.

Let us chase some horseradish and go fishing for seaweed— but I forgot I hadn't told you about the seafood.

You know about the *sulphur foods* already, but you get *Iodine* in anything (particularly shell fish) which comes out of the sea and *Silicone* from grain (barley, wheat, oats or rice) *with the husk on*—strawberries, cucumber peel, horseradish, asparagus, green figs, cabbage, lettuce and spinach.

That's enough about food. EXCEPT that to save the cost of rouge you'd better eat iron. And you don't need to be a Strong Woman in a circus to do it either.

What you need lady, is blood, and iron is the stuff to give it to you. "Spinach" you say at once. "Can't bear the stuff". But it's not the only one. Watercress is even better, plus raisins, dried figs, lentils, calves' liver, cabbage, dried apricots, green chicory or dandelion, parsley, grapefruit, onions, lettuce and dried prunes.

It's quite a list.

It's a pity if you can't be bothered to mess about with lentils and liver, but there is a way to eat your iron with no bother at all. Put equal quantities of dried prunes, apricots and raisins in a bowl, cover with water, a teaspoonful of lemon juice, and a tablespoonful of honey and forget about it for twenty-four hours.

Have it for breakfast with rye bread, and not only will it be delicious but in three weeks you will be a whole lot better looking, as well as better in health and temper.

But all this skin-talk is, as Mr. Salteena said, "but as piffle before the wind". There's worse to come.

I don't want you to be merely The Bride's Mother, you can make a pretty dish of yourself in your own right if you'll just listen. There must be something about you we can concentrate on to create a sensation, even if it's only your walk.

Are you properly articulated? Do you swing freely from the hips with knees straight, tummy and tail tucked in, and chin well up. I knew a girl who got married on that alone and used to practise hip-swinging for hours before her mirror, while holding on to the foot of the bed, so that she didn't swing herself flat on her face.

The result was so perfect that like all the greatest works of art and craft, it looked natural and spontaneous. It also looked like Garbo and a cheetah, and all her young men raved about her "lovely lope" even though it was the only thing she had.

You might think that to put one foot before the other and repeat ad. lib. or da capo was a natural and universal accomplishment, but with some it looks more natural than others and I have even read a recipe for it in an old book on deportment.

"To improve the walk, first find a straight line in the pattern of your rug, or in the boards of the floor or stretch a piece of string. Stand with your feet on the line, the left one a few inches in front of the right. Let your weight be evenly divided between the balls of your feet with your knees slightly flexed.

"Lift the right foot from the ground, raising the heel first, till only the toe touches. Then drag it lightly to the position of two inches in front of the left foot on the line, placing the toe down first.

"As the weights shifts from the toe (1) to the *ball* (2) of the forward foot (the right foot)", (Heaven help us, she isn't even taking two-inch steps now, she's progressing backwards) "raise the heel of the rear foot (the left foot) until the weight is on the toe, and then in turn place that foot in front of the forward foot."

Well I'm glad I know *how* it's done, but life, when you've run heedlessly through half of it, seems too brief to waste in complicated exercises like putting one foot before the other in small pieces and departmentalised confetti. It's like "painting by numbers" a picture of the Grand Canyon.

Go get me a canyon and I'll paint it as it stands. So will I walk.

Shorn of its precise instructions, it's merely a question of a free swing from the hip, a straight knee, a horizontal foot placed ball-first on the ground and the rest hardly touching at all, the weight of the body being very slightly forward of the vertical with chin and ball of foot in a straight line.

I think this limbering up stuff is all to the good and imparts so much youth and lightness to your step that The Child may very well catch on to it too, to her great betterment, and inquire how it's done. Anyone can do it in about six easy lessons and it's a pity that more people don't.

Do you ever *listen* to people walking? The brusque quick opinionated thump of a short, but probably quite light, woman, agony to listen to and shattering to her spine—the flat dogmatic tread of the brogued and worthy Committee member, who is probably not flat-footed at all, but has forgotten the use of her ankles and humps each leg along in one piece—the bent-kneed wooden click of the Smart-at-Any-Price, so destructive to both her nerves and ours—the sagging shiftless shuffle of the sandalled and the artless prance of the ballet-shoe-shod. (A sentence which will do equally well to water the geraniums or as a test for drunkenness.)

You can learn more from listening to footsteps than by looking at faces. You'd better listen to your own right now and see to it that they're not giving your age away.

Other exercises are a bore and rarely continued solo for more than a couple of half-hearted attempts, but if you and The Child form a Mutual Improvement Society you'll neither of you have the nerve to stop while the other has breath in her body. And once you begin to feel the benefit of this jolly P.T. you'll find yourself riding it as a hobby horse—full tilt at a great wallop. It's the quickest deportment-improver I know (I had it from a Guards P.T. instructor thirty years ago) and so tones up your muscles all over that you'll look a new woman.

Besides, whatever doctors say, it *will* improve your outline. There is a universal confusion of thought between over*weight* and over*size*. Mothers are afraid to say "fat", so they say "weight", which sounds more genteel and less alarming.

Doctors and Those who Diagnose, very rightly say that exercise sheds no weight and that you'd need to walk thirty miles (or something silly like that) to lose a pound. But if it's only *inches*, not *ounces*, that divide you from your daughter we can dwindle them and at the same time so tone you up all over that your eyes and hair shine, your skin clears, your muscles carry you competently and the insurance company knock a few £'s off your life-premium. Jump to it lady and you're saved.

Do it in the morning in your pyjamas, preferably before an open window, and if you can spend five minutes yawning and stretching as hard as you can stretch, before getting out of bed, so much the better.

1. Now, knees together and straight-legged, do the old toe-touching act six times, stretching *backwards* as far as possible with thumbs clasped as you breath *in* and breathing *out* as you go down towards your toes. Six times and no knee-bending, please.

2. Have you ever watched fencing?

Put yourself into a more-or-less fencing position—left knee bent, foot pointing outwards, left arm holding a beach-ball on the shoulder and face looking over left elbow, right arm hanging loosely by the right knee, holding an imaginary dumb bell.

Now raise right hand as far above your head as it will go, pretending that it is lifting a heavy weight. You can feel every muscle from neck to ankle getting its quota of exercise. And having raised your imaginary weight, slowly lower it again. Let's have this one six times and take it steady, then reverse the stance and do it all over again with the other arm. I know no exercise like this for toning up the muscles and yet, so far as I can discover, it has never been published.

3. Arms stretched wide, legs ditto, try to bend *side*ways and touch ankles, with legs and arms stiff, a good waist and rump whittler. Ten times slowly and always remembering to breathe *out* as you go down and *in* as you go up.

4. Legs as far apart as possible but arms joined above head this time. Bend, taut, and touch toes ten times each side. Tightens up the tummy.

5. Sit with legs wide apart and do the same, first touching one foot then returning to the upright and stretching over to the other. Six of each.

6. Legs apart, one slightly forward of the other, hands joined above head. Now bending sideways from the waist and keeping hips still, try to describe as big a circle *round yourself* as you can. Down to the right, across the front, round to the back and return. Make six circles in one direction, then swap the forward foot for the other one and do it in a reverse direction, always stretching outwards/forwards/backwards/sideways/as far as possible, in fact making a grand big circle.

7. Now, holding the knees and shoulders as rigid as possible, rotate the hips in as big a circle as you can. It's the old hulahula without the grass skirt, but done in slow motion and dead seriousness.

You can feel the good fresh air filling you in great gulps and the blood tearing about all over. It takes years off you in a month, and if your daughter won't play there are Health and Beauty classes everywhere all the time, with or without music. But I doubt whether they'll do these exercises, or whether the effect will be so swift.

For your jawline. Stretch your neck as high as it will go and your chin well out. Slowly and snootily turn your head and look as far backwards as you can over your left shoulder without screwing your head right off. Now reverse.

You can do this every time you are waiting for a kettle to

boil. You can even do it on the tube or on the street (in which case you can take a hat round the crowd and afterwards explain that you are rehearsing for your part as 1st ostrich in the next pantomime).

About the house, if you have to lift, stretch, or bend, then bend like blazes for your muscles' sake. Even sitting can be an exercise if you tuck your tail properly into the angle of an upright chair where seat joins back, keep your shoulders well back and down and your chin up.

It's the way our grandmothers used to sit, and after all, if our rear end was given us to sit on why use the shoulder blades?

This is one case where you will be not only in step but way out ahead of the lounging child. So make the most of it.

VII

This Too, Too Solid Flesh, with some Chat about Calories

THE WAILS of the worried in this matter have resounded since Hamlet first broached the subject. "Oh!" he cried, "that this too, too solid flesh would melt", and a large section of the public have been crying it ever since. But I may be able to help you.

An amateur in most subjects, I claim to speak with authority on this one, having for twenty years sampled, sunk under or merely sniffed at, every diet that was ever invented and quite a few that haven't been thought up yet.

The resolution to do better today is born anew every morning and Hope, as the Poet says, springs eternal in the human breast. Ah well! If it achieves nothing else, hope keeps you young and active. So long as you're *doing* something about it, all is not lost. But you'd better do *something*.

There is no physical factor which so accentuates the gulf between mother and daughter as a difference of forty pounds in weight. You can't possibly keep pace with her if she skips like the young lambs and you wallow after her like the mutton that you are. Even when you've upholstered your rather regrettable chassis with what the French call "etincillante carrosserie" (sparkling coachwork) you can't get away with it.

But though you may be over forty (both in age and two out of three of your "vital statistics") don't despair. We can fix it one way or another. In fact we're *going* to fix it or perish in the attempt.

You can take it from me as an old diet-hound that excess weight (oh hell! Let's call it "fat", I've got to keep the words down to a minimum in this thing), whatever fancy-work you like to put in on your alibi, comes from wrong habits of eating or drinking or a bit of both.

Can you remember your appearance at seventeen? Well you've still got the same skeleton haven't you? Only you can't see it. It's all this stuff that Time has superimposed on it that has altered your geography and if you really *want* to there's no reason (except your slackness, lack of will power, procrastination and private greeds) why you shouldn't.

I have been in close contact for some time with a specialist on obesity who is putting all his specialism in a book and has analysed about 1,000 of his case histories with remarkable results. No madam, there will be no names in it and even if you are one of his most interesting patients you are only a guinea-pig and utterly anonymous.

E

There is always a preliminary disclaimer of responsibility, says the doctor:

"My food does me more good than most people's."

"It is hereditary, my family are all fat."

"I am too cheerful, I don't worry enough."

"I mustn't go on a protein diet because of my blood pressure."

"I mustn't take much exercise because of my heart."

"The trouble is glandular, pituitary or thyroid or something."

"I mustn't reduce because I am a busy woman and it saps one's energy."

"I eat like a bird but it all turns to fat."

"Dieting makes one so irritable and my family *do* so enjoy my cheerful disposition."

"It's my metabolism, doctor, it's not burning up my food properly."

"I never touch sugar, fat, starch or alcohol, it's just a middle-aged spread and you can't cure it."

And so on. Not one half of one per cent has any truth in it, and the glandular deficiency, the most popular alibi of all, shifting the responsibility squarely on to one's make-up and off oneself, is the biggest humbug of all.

Certainly there are various reasons for this insidious uphol-stery which is slowly smothering us. Reasons which might be slow to appear and difficult to dig out, but most of them sooner or later are connected with an intake of surplus calories and their conversion into unseemly rolls and pillows where in the best statuary none exists.

Are you worried for instance? You could even be worried about The Child—her fast friends/driving/expenditure/behaviour/increasing independence, or her slow acquisition of responsibility/useful knowledge/a hobby/a career/academic attainments/sense/discrimination.

Even though you can't do a thing about it, you get all tensed up, and in order to distract your mind you have a cocktail or nibble petits fours, or go to a party, or out to lunch with some crony to whom you can unburden yourself over a delicious menu.

You feel *impelled* towards one of these courses as a distraction, and you can't eliminate the nervous "stoking-up" without increasing the nervous strain.

It just won't do, you know, and since it takes an extremely honest mum to discover for herself these basic beginnings of obesity in unlikely causes, I advise you to consult a doctor who will do the digging for you.

"No man can be trusted to give a report on his own well-being", said a philosopher whose name eludes me, and it applies even more so to women. Get a neutral referee to decide what is lying so heavily on your sub-conscious.

Are you afraid?

Overdraft? Claustrophobia? Old age? Airplanes? Life? Death? Hunting? Ski-ing? Being fat? Atom bombs? People? Spiders or the dark?

Not only will you be nibbling to relax your nerves, the blood will be busy in your head helping you to worry, instead of in your body helping to burn up the nibbles.

It could even be that you were bored (home, job, husband, daughter, routine, or lack of any of these), or have an inferiority complex (about any of the above). The first step in a cure is confession, the next relaxation, the next reformation, and in all of these the doctor will assist, by tablets to stave off a too hearty intake—to step up the fuel disposal rate—to calm the nerves—to aid elimination—to bestow new energy. Aids which are at least half the answer to the trouble.

The rest is up to you.

Everybody now knows that various foods contain varying

amounts of calories—a calorie being merely a measurement in terms of heat—the amount of fuel required to raise the temperature of a pint of water 4°F.

Calories come from the three main elements of food, fats, proteins and carbohydrates, and the game is to combine them in such a form that you have a properly varied diet with enough calories to burn up your waste products, keep you warm and provide energy, enough bulk to satisfy appetite, and enough vitamins and minerals to keep you healthy. Excess calories of carbohydrates are stored as fat—excess calories in fat go to the same places only rather quicker, but proteins speed the burning-up process, increase energy, and generally tone up the metabolism.

Which is why, to the fat, protein foods are life savers and loom large in the diet. I'm sorry all this theory is so boring but *someone* has to elucidate that word "calorie", which is bandied about in every woman's magazine, without ever being explained, until you would think it was something that should be abolished by Act of Parliament or rat-poison.

The main proteins are lean meat and poultry, liver, lentils, peas, oysters, eggs, yoghurt and cottage cheese, so you can help yourself. It's no use cutting out completely all fats and carbohydrates, you need them for warmth and vitamins (particularly the dairy fats like milk and cheese) but if you keep to a high protein, low starch, low fat régime and have some of each food group daily, you will not only melt the too-too-solid flesh but become younger and more like your daughter every day.

There is no need to stick to a hard and fast menu. I shan't attempt to outline three meals a day for all the days of the week.

Man (and even more particularly woman) does not live by calories alone and if you have any special food fads you can probably indulge them within the range of reasonable foods. But you'll have to lay off some of the others to even things up.

And if you know the foods which are packed and crammed with calories as distinct from those which are equally filling but less dangerous you can pick your way about, tiptoeing nicely round the pitfalls and being a real devil with parsnips and artichokes.

On the other hand, if you don't care for bits of information about forbidden fruit—if it destroys all your pleasures and makes life a desert, you can skip the lot and join us later.

Personally, seeing that you've paid for the book and it's the only bit of genuine science in the whole thing, done by a friend who helped me with the hard bits, I should have a go and get your money's worth.

Here, briefly, is the diet sheet which almost every doctor will give you.

1. Eat or drink as much as you like (or can get) of:—

Lean meat, poultry, game, rabbit, hare, liver, kidney, heart, sweetbread—cooked in any way without addition of flour, breadcrumbs or thick sauces.

Fish (not tinned)—boiled or steamed only, no thick sauce. Eggs, boiled or poached only.

Potatoes, boiled, steamed, or baked in their skins, but not fried, roast, sauté or "chips" and not potato powder.

Other vegetables of all kinds (fresh, tinned or dried) cooked in any way not involving the use of fat.

Salad and tomatoes *without* oil or mayonnaise.

Beetroot, radishes, watercress, parsley.

Fresh fruit of any kind including bananas. Also bottled fruit —if bottled without sugar. Not tinned or dried fruits (including dates, figs and raisins) because of the concentration of sugar.

Sour pickles, not sweet pickles or chutneys.

Clear soup, broth, "Bovril", "Oxo", "Marmite".

Salt, pepper, mustard, vinegar, Worcester sauce. No other sauces.

Saccharin or saxin for sweetening.

Water, soda-water and non-sweetened mineral waters.

Tea and coffee (milk only as allowed below).

2. You may have milk (not condensed) up to half a pint daily. No cream.

3. You may have three very small pieces of bread per day and take them either one at each meal or all three at one meal as desired. (Very small means not exceeding one ounce each, which is one slice from a cut-loaf).

4. You may have nothing else whatever: particularly note that this means:—

No butter, margarine, fat or oil (except for cooking meat NOT fish).

No sugar, honey, jam, marmalade, sweets, chocolate, cocoa. No puddings, ices, dried or tinned fruits, nuts.

No bread (except as above) cake, biscuits, toast, patent reducing breads, cereals, oatmeal, "All-Bran", "Ryvita", "Vitabread".

No barley, rice, macaroni, spaghetti, semolina, sausages, cheese.

No cocktail savouries, alcohol (beer, cider, wines and spirits).

WEIGH BEFORE YOU BEGIN AND THEREAFTER WEEKLY ON THE *SAME SCALES* IN THE *SAME CLOTHES* AND AT THE *SAME TIME* OF DAY.

Actually it was The Child who gave the diet chart to me, and probably your own has studied it too. They are usually only too pleased to co-operate in this matter of keeping pace and eager to see you as lithe and comely as themselves.

Alas, for us it is more difficult.

Any daughter who really gets her teeth into this diet and doesn't cheat can lose 14 lbs. in a month and look and feel all the better for it—full of vim and vigour.

Any middle-aged mamma is more likely to take four to six months and if she tries to shed the surplus more quickly she'll look a hag and be a nervous wreck. But it's a pretty reasonable diet, as diets go, and you won't be hungry on it, even if you're sometimes a trifle bored.

The inclusion of bananas may surprise you. Me too. They have always hitherto been regarded as having a very injurious effect on one's outline. But when we get down to statistics it seems that a baked apple has 145 calories and a banana only 109, of which 100 are carbohydrates and plumb full of energy. So you can take your choice.

Fresh pineapple, grapefruit and strawberries all rank pretty low in calories, but beware of the tinned kind, they're certain sure to be done in sugar. I mention fruit particularly because it's stuffed brim-full of all the little-things-that-count—minerals and vitamins and odds and bits of things that do you good all over.

You see by the diet sheet that even potatoes aren't banned though they rate 170 calories per large-baked-in-jacket against twenty for an equal weight of artichokes and four (I repeat four) for parsnips. But potatoes are some of the finest energy foods in existence, owing to their high carbohydrate content and parsnips have none at all. So help yourself to whichever you fancy.

But oh the awful potency of chips or crisps! My doctor tells me they work out at about ten calories apiece and when you're trying to keep to a daily minimum of about 1,250 it's hardly worth the expenditure.

Veal at about 110 calories is the best meat, liver roughly the same, and rabbit slightly higher. Beef of any kind is heavier on calories, but it's a high-protein food which means that the calories are burning up not only themselves but others too and therefore a steak is the staple food of most slimmers.

But *grilled* you understand, not fried, because of the fat.

Theoretically you could live on this and green vegetables. Actually after a week you'd be dead sick of it, decide to call off the experiment and eat either everything or nothing.

Unfortunately it's possible to cheat.

It is understood between us that any average helping of meat is four ounces and one of vegetables half a breakfast cup. If your diet sheet says "one mutton chop with beans, one pat butter, quarter pineapple", who is going to weigh a sloppy mess of Scarlet Runners? And it is well known that chops, pats, and pineapples, come in all sizes.

Take fish now.

You might think that fish was pretty harmless. Harm, so far as I can see, going frequently hand-in-hand with flavour. But what about some of the more appetising fishes, say tunny at 250 calories, 150 of which are fat? Salmon only slightly less, mackerel 400 each and herrings and kippers 300. It's the oil of course.

I suppose they need all that greasy stuff, like whales and

swimmers do, to keep the seawater out. But any white fish (cod, whiting, plaice, haddock) (steamed!) and without salt (!!) will use only 150 calories for a nice slab, tasting and looking like pure cotton wool, though if you doll it up with a few mushrooms, tomatoes, rings of onion and drops of lemon juice, you can call it Continental Cooking and no-one will know or care.

But you've *got* to be in a state where you don't care, to appreciate steamed cod.

To fry it would boost that identical fillet to 250 and then

out of pure habit you'd add a dozen or so chips and some sauce and there we are.

Well, *where* are we?

About 400 on the road to damnation again.

We will talk of bread and all floury products with bated breath. Better not talk of them at all, but three ounces a day (3 slices of a ready-cut loaf) taken either all together or separately, won't hurt. It's mostly carbohydrate (and therefore potential energy) and it doesn't matter whether it's white or brown, toasted or fresh, patent-starch-reduced or home-made. The flour is the trouble every time. Plain white flour rates 340 calories of carbohydrates, 50 of protein and 10 of fat, a total of 400 per half-pound and we can therefore not afford to toy with any flour products whatever. No sauce, no thick soup, no thickened gravies, no pancakes, muffins, macaroons, cereals, biscuits, rolls, cakes or pastry.

One wedge of Devil's food cake (chocolate sandwich iced) which anyone is liable to eat almost without knowing it, would set you back 400 calories, and the meanest sort of doughnut 230. Think of it! Two slices of cake and doughnut with a cup of café creme and you've had your day's food and drink.

A rectangle of gingerbread costs 200 even if without dried fruit, and apple pie 200 for a four ounce serving. Mince pie costs you 100 calories per ounce which is the cruellest blow of all.

I suppose it's all that dried fruit, suet and gummy, rummy, syrupy, embellishment that makes it so dangerous. But when I think of all the delicious hot and spicy mince pies—as likely as not topped with a thick blob of genuine cream—that I have eaten in my life—I could weep that they are forbidden for evermore.

So far as I can see *everything* is forbidden at Christmas. Alcohol is wildly fattening and soft drinks almost as bad. Though that doesn't mean an end to all party-going. "Dost thou think," said Shakespeare, "dost thou think that, because thou art virtuous, there shall be no more cakes and ale?" But if you exceed your allowance somewhat today do try to knock off a little extra tomorrow and be as prudent as possible with your jollifications. You'll have to get used to having tomato juice cocktails (25 calories per small glass) not even tinned fruit juice, because it's always sweetened, and rates seventy–ninety.

Brazils are terrible for the torso, two will cost you a hundred calories; plum-pudding is the upholsterer par excellence; rum sauce right out; potatoes in, only if baked or plain boiled, and we can't even have chestnuts with the sprouts. A nice floury chestnut being worth roughly the same as an artichoke.

Though who *wants* to sit round the Christmas fire roasting artichokes, and watching the young and slender ones guzzling chocolate liqueurs and plum cake with an inch thick layer of almond icing?

This is all too morbid.

Let's look at something constructive for a change. It was necessary to shock you first and I can now apply some consolation in the shape of rewards for your good conduct.

If you are a housewife, which is regarded by doctors—entirely without reason—as a sedentary occupation, and are thirty pounds overweight, you should lose one and a half pounds a week on the special diet and that's plenty. You don't want your skin to go wrinkled and baggy like an old elephant do you? Well it *will* if you unstuff it too quickly.

Use saccharine or saxin for sweetening and pour off the top of the milk, using only the skim. Keep drink (of any sort, because even the soft ones are sweet) down to one and a half pints a day if possible, of which only half a pint should be milk. And don't drink *with* meals, only *between*. You may be a "human sponge", one of

the water-retaining people who tuck away an undue proportion of their intake just where it's least ornamental.

You're not a camel and you don't need it, so try to use it up by drinking less and if you think you're not getting rid of enough, consult your doctor, who can speed up your rate of discharge by harmless diuretic tablets as easily as he could prescribe a laxative.

By the way I suppose *that* department is functioning well? Just check up before beginning your diet and take a good dose of something (Epsom or other salts) two mornings running in case anything has got left behind in the corners.

And you'd better beware all "wet" foods, leeks, greens, cherries, grapes, for example. Liquids of the wrong sort, or in excess, can be as dangerous to your line as solids. Salt too. It helps to hold liquid in suspension in the human frame, so keep your mouth shut when bathing and never add salt to cooked foods except boiled eggs.

Do eat at least one egg a day, it's good protein and at seventy-five apiece they are good value, but if you want *more* than one have one-and-a-white, whites counting fifteen and yolks sixty. No I *know* you can't boil a white, madam, but what's wrong with scrambling it with a dash of Worcester sauce or making a baked custard. The cinnamon is free.

Well! That's taken care of the ordinary meals, but what about snacks. They may be only a nervous habit, but it's a habit that, once acquired, is singularly difficult to break.

Gayelord Hauser suggests that when you are watching television you should have a tray of delicious juicy carrots handy to nibble when your stomach calls.

Every man to his poison and carrots just aren't mine. Unfortunately my special poison is petits fours, made of almond paste, just deliciously browned and crisp, with maybe a walnut on—oh, I can't bear it! Hand me an apple to get my teeth into.

There's nothing wrong with an apple is there? As juicy as a carrot with a much more refined taste, and if slightly more costly in calories we've got to break out a little sometimes.

A man I knew advocated those exceptionally large and hard kind of peppermint bull's-eyes, known to the humble child as gob-stoppers (and not without cause) as a mind-distractor of the first water. He said that with one of these he could kid himself for hours that he was eating something.

All I can say is that his powers of self-deception are excessively well-developed and it was his mind that needed treatment as urgently as his embonpoint. The only time I ever tried it I was involved in a sudden outbreak of hiccoughs and only by standing me on my head and bouncing me—like mad —was the stopper unstopped.

May I recommend chewing gum as being more manageable? If you are going to masticate anything (and, by gum! I believe that is where the word comes from, mastic being putty!) choose something soft.

A re-cap now, then go right into the kitchen for a bit of practice.

Do eat slowly and chew well. It lasts longer and you get bored sooner.

Do have an apple or a salad to begin a meal, you'll never get as far as the sweet and remember that ten ounces of turnips equal one ounce of bread.

Do get some reliable scales and heed what they say.

Do cut all fat off your meat.

Do use saxin instead of sugar.

Do keep to *lean* poultry, ham, fish and meat.

Do remember that one teaspoonful of salt holds one pint of

water in your tissues. It's quite possible that without it you'd be lean and comely.

Do cut out starches and nearly all butter.

Do throw away the frying-pan and grill everything.

And finally do eat salad with cottage cheese and yoghurt whenever possible. The former rates sixty and the latter only fifteen a helping.

The very nicest salads I know mix green food, fruit, vegetables and cottage cheese in reckless profusion and you should have one every day.

To cook summer fruit without sugar, use a pinch of bicarbonate, to neutralise some of its acid, and then add saxin afterwards. But really it's much better and goes much further, eaten raw.

You can try a milk and banana, milk and apple, or milk and potato diet for two days a week if you like. A little of what you fancy does you good. But except as a change of diet it really doesn't do you *much* good. It's a purely temporary weight-shedder. And its main drawback is that there's nothing to prepare, and therefore too much time left on your hands in which you can think about all the nice things you are missing.

If you fix yourself a good mixed diet from some of the permitted foods on the chart, precede it with a salad and top it with a slice of pineapple or a pear, you will be so busy that there will be no time left for thinking about anything.

And, as we said in the beginning, the less you *think* and the more you *do*, the quicker the flesh will melt. Probably in no time at all The Child will be poring over your diet sheets in the endeavour to keep pace with her mamma.

VIII

Friends, Hers, Mine and Ours

How much interest should you take in the Child's men-friends and she in yours?

I would say in either case, not too much or too obviously.

Her evanescent love affairs may, if by good behaviour you have earned the right to such confidence, be made visible before your eyes. They will rarely be discussed.

She will from time to time casually produce a young man for your inspection but you are not intended to make any report on your findings, or even to find them. You must be as elaborately casual as themselves—see all, know all and say nothing.

There is an Arabian proverb to the effect that "The camel-driver has his thoughts and the camel also," but it seems to be understood that neither intrudes upon those of the other.

Everyone is entitled to their mental privacy, the young most of all, and if you expect to share all her thoughts and friendships you're going to be disappointed.

She is perhaps conscious that her judgement in respect of boy friends is likely to be a trifle biased and that if he is utterly beyond the pale and you have seen him, the responsibility is yours not hers. But your judgement must be reserved until called for, which will probably be never, and not offered gratis.

Far from keeping her at home, you must *encourage* her to meet the other sex—create opportunities—be unfailingly pleasant even when you think they're cads, wolves, nincompoops, howling outsiders.

One harsh word from you and she'll toughen up, and, out of pure obstinacy and the inner need for power over her own destiny, defend them to the last drop of her blood. Much better encourage it and let her sicken of them naturally—as she will do, given time, if you've brought her up to have balance and discrimination.

And if after a few starts, she seems to be taking too seriously some slightly substandard candidate, it is as well to have a few alternatives up your sleeve and proffer them as casually as she.

After all, the current "he" may not be deformed, depraved or devoid of table manners, merely dull, and her devotion has blinded both her and him to the fact.

"All dullness is in the mind; it comes out thence and diffuses itself over everything round the dull person and then he terms everything dull and thinks himself the victim of the impact of dull things," wrote C. E. Montague, which appears to apply very closely to a nit-witted adolescent. Alone with her she may think him strong and silent, or perhaps just silent, but against the background of home life he is seen to have no spark of intelligence because there is nothing in him from which to strike one.

Beware of expressing any such opinion. It will make her cleave the closer in sympathy. If you produce one or two boys with one or two ideas it should be sufficient to point a contrast. The definition of male education used to be that a boy

must be able to entertain himself, a stranger, and a new idea, disability in any of these respects being deemed a serious matter.

My own severe test for the Young Unknown at first meetings was to get him in a corner and project some outlandish topic as soon as possible, whether it was ghosts—gardening—geology in gravel pits—goat-breeding—grovelling under car bonnets or gold digging in Alaska. With a top score of ten, any response at all earned one mark a minute, an intelligent response two and an eager one three, with a mental danger sign and Go Slow notices over the last because over-enthusiasm in a Mother can be a severe handicap to a daughter.

Nevertheless if there is some topic on which you and she and her friends can all be interested, whether it's apple picking or interior decorating or collecting stamps, you're a lucky woman and she's a lucky girl. The relationship will be delightful whether permanent or not and you will be able to remain beside her during the selective process, taking silent notes.

I'm not suggesting that you should accompany her to parties, such co-ordination of movement smacks to me of parental supervision and as such is very repugnant to the young. After all she's not a child now.

No less a Body than the Ministry of Pensions and National Insurance so clearly lays it down that "In determining whether a person is a child, the prime consideration is his age", that there is no doubt upon the matter. You must therefore take up your role of Background, something against which the young woman can pose the boy of the moment to see how he looks, and otherwise you can be of no use at all.

I don't even suggest that you appear at your own parties, except in small doses, intermittently, and before the dancing begins. It's likely to get rougher after.

And if she goes out alone to parties, let her go and don't nag. They're all doing it now and she hates to feel she's different from the rest. What do you *expect* her to be doing? Dalcroze eurythmics in a gym tunic?

There is very little vice in youth and a lot of hot air circulated about it. Their dance bands make a noise and the Press makes another one, but it's the modern atmosphere—*their* atmosphere and it would be highly inconsistent to expect them to behave other than as they do.

Last winter there was a wave of parental horror and Press hot-air about some dance called a Creep. It was apparently as decadent as a slow-moving dervish dance of Hottentots, who, having parked their assegais in the cloakroom, gyrated eerily round a human sacrifice in their full funeral regalia. If there had been skeletons, or witchcraft in it somewhere I wouldn't have been surprised.

If they had been *drunken* dancers, *doped* dancers or only ghouls who *looked* like dancers and were actually practitioners in Black Markets, Black Masses and Black Magic, it would not have astonished me, but in fact I could see nothing decadent in this slow amble round a small hot room, while three men moaned on curvaceous brass, one plucked steel strings, one padded gently on small drums, and a sixth rode a bucking double bass.

Never a sniff of brimstone anywhere. It was not decadent. It was only dull. They didn't even lower the lights! And they were drinking nothing but coffee!!

The low-down on all parental disapproval is that it's part of the act. We old ones enjoy finding something at which to be shocked, amazed and if possible a little hurt, under the impression that it boosts our authority.

But do you remember the 1920's lady? It's all Cartier's to a Woolworth what-not that you were a deb yourself in that unbuttoned era. Do you remember the Charleston or the Black Bottom? Did you or did you not (no cheating now) ooze round a semi-lit ballroom in a semi-conscious state and a short pink sack all sickled o'er with fringe.

We were Vamps that year. Concave houris with Grecian hair-bands, long jetty eyelashes, scarlet mouths and foot-long cigarette-holders, and some of the most unctuous and passion-provoking gargles that ever trembled from a trumpet or swooned from a sax kept us circling in dead-slow motion round the floor.

Creep indeed! They don't know a thing!

If you gyrated, clamped to the shirt front of the current boy-friend, at the rate of half-a-mile-an-hour you were a fast mover, and a girl I knew (now a haughty peeress) invariably concealed a small alarm clock in her corsage lest she fell asleep negotiating a corner in the early hours.

Play fair, madam, and before turning your nose up or your thumbs down at some current pursuit, alleged to be decadent, think back to yourself at the same age.

They're only playing at being grown-up, to conceal from a censorious world their tender youth, and terrible inexperience, and this bloodcurdling veneer of sophistication is part of the game—make-up, eye-shadow, talons and all.

They're her battle array, the tools of her trade. We called them "glad rags" but they were just the same.

You see what I mean?

There is a theory that no Nice Girl ever Pursues a Man. Indeed, some titled woman with a brace of daughters said that very thing under enormous headlines last week.

Boloney! Pure and utter boloney. The proper study of Woman is Man, as John Stuart Mill almost said. She has always pursued him and always will, be the pronouncements of peeresses what they may.

True, the manner and degree of the female pursuit vary as much as the pace of the male recession. It is a perfectly comprehended and properly conducted process (on both sides) for the furtherance of Nature's programme, and, artistically performed, it might be difficult for a casual onlooker to decide who is chasing whom.

The victim-designate flutters her lure. The keen, tight-feathered falcon stoops, makes his strike and proudly bears off his prize to the eyrie (with television and all mod. con.) that he has prepared for her, on yonder rock.

But who first drew his attention to the prey, I ask you? And the answer is the Prey herself who first dropped a glove, as a guerdon for a knight's helmet and a challenge to him to snaffle the dropper. It's the fluttering Victim again.

No, the Female is the Huntress, whatever the art and craft of her dissembling. Which is very right and proper, so long as she keeps him in ignorance of the fact.

Of course men have to be chased.

My Mother once had a housemaid from school-leaving to pensioning-off age, but it looked for about twelve years in the middle as if we were going to lose her. She was "walking-out" with a bricklayer (the recognized stage between, "a-talkin'-to" and "a-courtin'-of", all necessary preliminaries to a ring and a marriage, though not necessarily to a family).

We don't rush things in the country.

Anyhow walking-out it was, on her evening off, four miles out to look at his mother's grave (and four miles back) with never a word spoken on either side. But one evening when the affair was rising up for thirteen years, the weight of heavy thoughts crashed through the barrier of speech and he said "Bread's riz". A perfectly comprehended commentary on the fact that the rising cost of life's basic essential now put any question of marriage beyond the economic pale. And what a lot of words we waste on simple facts. "Bread's riz," to me, has a kind of poignant poetry about it. You couldn't detract a syllable and still be coherent, which is one of the acid tests.

So Hannah relinquished her idea of orange blossom without a struggle and they never walked again, whereas with a little chasing she might have landed him. They could always, like the subjects of Louis XVI, have lived on cake.

Even Jacob, after some preliminary jiggery-pokery with the Sister of the Bride (there was no electric lighting in the tents of Laban) got Rachel in the end, and I can't think why she allowed him to do fourteen years' hard labour before the wedding ceremony. Girls had no grit in those days, Hannah had no grit either, and I thank the gods of Reason that our daughters have so far reverted to nature as to out and club their man on the head if they want him and bring home the body to mamma to be certified as a Grade A exhibit, while he

murmurs feebly, "I'm awfully struck by your daughter", a juster mot than he wots of.

Sometimes one thinks it's the *Daughter* who should be certified, but that's *her* show. He's not marrying both of you. Indeed sometimes it is problematical as to whether he's marrying *either* of you. But keep out, it's her funeral. No comments, no comparisons, no cagey remarks, no crying. You are in danger of forgetting that she is a Person, not a mere echo, and the best thing to do is to stand back and let her make her own selections.

In order to keep pace with the poor girl in those tremulous, delicate, difficult days before engagement you must remain fluid and adaptable, move with the times and forbear any heavy pontifical judgements on her manners, customs, cronies, or accoutrements however startling they may appear. You might, as she proceeds with your higher (and wider) education be obliged to eat your words, and they'd be heavier than ever then.

Daughters come in several kinds and their parents react to them in sundry ways, but your one sure line is never to show surprise.

Play for safety every time and express no alarm. And if you refuse to be shocked when she goes to the Platelayers' Ball with an engine greaser she will abandon the attempt to shock you. If you suggest asking him to your next cocktail party she will abandon the greaser. You have taken her for better or worse (you had to) but it is largely up to you to ensure how *much* better or worse it is.

When she finds that the temperature is bland and that her high spirits cut no ice because there's no ice to cut, she'll stop acting, throw away her mask and you can begin having some real fun as two real people.

But what if you don't *want* to have fun together? If you

are too static, too shy, too bored, to get any joy from invitations?

You should really bestir yourself, you know, and take advantage of this unique opportunity. It's probably your last dual appearance at any function—except of course her wedding. You can always arrange some family code to signal when a mutual friend has offered to put an end to your misery by running you home and leave her to be escorted later.

But be careful not to enjoy it too much. If the thing has turned sour on her, as parties sometimes do—the right man is absent, the wrong one too prevalent and herself suffering brilliant hardships with a set smile—you must abandon all. Even if a long-lost charmer of your youth has just begged for the supper dance you must agree with her that your feet are killing you and take her home.

If you're shy that's nothing. You immediately pick out someone even shyer than yourself who knows less people and try to put them at their ease. Repeat ad lib.

But there is one painful necessity on all occasions when you are allowed to accompany her. You must allow *her* to decide what you may wear.

"But my *dear*," she says in horror, "you look exactly like Madame Marcati in that black thing with jade ear-rings!"

No hope now for those ancient and outrageous garments of which it is frequently impossible to tell date/object/colour/back/front, or even whether they were meant to be worn or waved. They must be sacrificed to her good taste and you will be well advised to put yourself unreservedly in her hands.

Who will advise you to do so?

She will of course.

As to her attitude to *your* men friends.

It's naturally somewhat galling when she dislikes them, finds flaws in them that you haven't seen and pointedly removes herself from their company. But it's not always (not altogether) jealousy.

A second diagnostic opinion is always valuable and need not necessarily be from a specialist, a general practitioner will do. There are so many specialists already and not enough all-rounders to go all round. So I think ones wisest course is to be thankful for her common sense, her acute judgement and wide experience and once more let her decide.

And if she says "I don't think he's *quite* your line of country, mummy", it's heavy odds that she's right.

IX

It's Her Show Now

THE middle and late teens are the time when physical and mental agility are of utmost value to the aspiring and perspiring parent.

If you only knew where she was—mentally or spiritually—at this stage, you could do something concrete about keeping pace with her, but when life is a perpetual contra-dance, with the pair of you swapping sides daily, the best you can hope for is to retain sufficient fluidity to follow her lead.

It is like accompanying on the piano a concert singer who can't hold her pitch. What's the use of ferociously thumbing middle C in the effort to recall her? She's oblivious, and only the audience, against whom you are *both* in league, is aware of the conflict.

You may not both be *absolutely* on the same note but so long as she can retain a vague impression that you are somewhere in the background, more or less *with* her, there will be an aura of comfort and security about the association, and together you may well so puzzle the world that they hail it as a piece of exquisite artistry.

The art of "accompanying by ear" is never more desperately needed than in these late "teens".

You have been conditioned by the Child to be utterly conventional. You and she must look, and behave, exactly as a thousand of her contemporaries do—a protective coloration much indulged in by animals and excruciatingly familiar to mothers of middle-sized boys at Public Schools, where it reaches its most feverish phase.

They are not *ready* yet to be Individuals therefore *you* must not be an individual. There is a Common Denominator for parents, a kind of pattern and Totem to which they bow, and if you deviate one iota out of the shadow of this Awful Fetish you have brought distinction and therefore disgrace on both of you.

You wonder where you've gone wrong. How can they be such little idiots as to believe that your hat (it's usually a hat), your car, your choice of nail lacquer, your dog, your career, even your small-talk must be so played down as to conform to all the rest, and that to be distinguished is to be damned.

But bless their little hearts. All they want is to be allowed to develop quietly behind their smoke screen of convention-ality, among an indistinguishable herd of other conventiona-lists, until they are ready to emerge, a mature and integrated personality, poised and delightful.

For heaven's sake don't stage a Parental Revolution. If that's their game you must play it too. Lie low and say nothing.

Being a parent is as much a distinguished career as any other and you must pay due attention to its science and intricacies. You may keep your own private notions about their absurdities but you must never air them.

Your only hope of pulling her out with dignity is to follow where she leads and make it sound as if it was planned that way.

You've got to discard the printed stuff and play it by ear.

Last week Mr. Chuter Ede, M.P., said "There are occasions when this House has to say that a certain thing is right, even if public opinion may not at the moment, be of the same opinion". And you have to stand by her and back her up, letting the devil look after public opinion.

If you are patient you will find that at about seventeen The Child suddenly cracks the chrysalis of conformity and emerges as a butterfly, to your utter dazzlement.

Where did she *get* these new notions? While she was taking cover behind the trivial pattern of her particular gang she must have used its quiet obscurity as a hatching ground for some excessively colourful ideas.

You are now, overnight, on the other foot, hopping violently to maintain your balance and to keep pace with her leaping performance.

She knows more about almost anything—the position of the Atacama desert/the conjugation of *assessoir*/the date of Charlemagne/the treatment of burns or viburnum/the times of train connections in foreign capitals/the cure for a hangover/the correct complementary colour for a lettuce-green frock—than *you* ever did or will. (The answer to the last being, so far as I remember, "Why, mayonnaise colour of course!")

Moreover, it seems that all things which are not in books but learned by the light of heaven alone—all sympathy, all resourcefulness, all courage and optimism and adventure—are also known to her. You pray hastily that you will get your second wind in time to be a fit companion.

But all the jumping about—the changes of mood and manners, ideas and ideals, with which you have kept pace for so long have been good training.

After the many "sink or swim" episodes of earlier years you find that together you are at the centre of the whirlpool. Jointly you struggle to terra firma. With a mighty heave you pull yourselves on to the bank, to find that she is an odd, unconventional, and adult friend, with a range of potentialities which is infinite.

What to do with her then? Because both she and you must do something.

The sole object of work is not financial reward. Chaliapin, in fact, declared that "No work can be fruitful if it has not as its basis, some ideal principle", and no less an authority than the American Declaration of Independence lays it down that "All men . . . are endowed by their Creator with inalienable rights, among which are life, liberty, and the pursuit of happiness".

Furthermore Bertrand Russell has it that "It is impossible to be happy without activity, but it is also impossible to be happy if the activity is excessive or of a repulsive kind. Activity is agreeable when it is directed very obviously to a desired end, and is not in itself contrary to impulse".

Which to me gives the direct information that the child must have work to do, but not necessarily the work which brings in the most money or the most fame. It must have some principle or ideal as its base and must be congenial, because it is her right to be happy in it.

Doubtless one could also prove by judicious selection from weighty authorities that work *itself* was the end, or, contrariwise, that only uncongenial, mechanical and well-paid work was worthwhile, because it would leave the mind free and the pocket well lined. It being well known that with a free mind and a good bank balance one can do almost anything, almost anywhere.

But I prefer to think that too much stress is laid on success in competition and getting to high places in record time.

From the date of the "11-plus" examination, Authority seems to have its criteria slightly misplaced. It has a tendency to hound this malleable material of youth into safe and sane occupations—to look too far ahead—to take too much thought for the morrow and canalise them firmly towards some inescapable end.

But how can one decide what is meat and drink to the young mind or how to guide their reluctant feet into paths where we can walk beside them?

The customary educational offerings of a girls' school suggest no very appropriate outcome.

"What do you want her to be?" gropes the Head Mistress, but her gropings are as nothing to the miasmic wanderings of our own bemused minds.

"Herself," you hopefully suggest, which is not, for some reason, considered to be a concrete proposal and you are obliged to dip in the bag again.

"If she could perhaps learn to speak French and the truth, play the piano, be patient with children and stand on her own feet?" you hazard tentatively and are very properly hailed as a jester.

That isn't a *career*, it's a backwater.

There isn't an academic hope or a prospect of laurels in it anywhere.

And yet, ten years later, you reap with joy and comfort the seeds so diffidently sown. The miracle has been accomplished unaided, and, among a bunch of specialists, the incompetent and unworthy mother is presented with the one non-conformist child, the one who has, either aggressively or absentmindedly, omitted to specialise and is therefore still capable of many things.

Now this is a ticklish stage and you mustn't push her.

Let her find her own line, follow her own inclination and if, for the moment, there appear to be *no* inclinations, cultivate her as a good companion. You will be doing some man a good turn eventually.

She may have some notion about a career. But, however hairbrained it may seem, never decry it. Study it yourself and try to share her interest. And when that wanes be prepared to drop it like a hot brick and jump ahead to the next.

It's being so lively that keeps you young.

She may exasperate you, tease you, puzzle you, possibly even destroy you, but she will never bore you. And all the time she is slowly wending her way, like a river to the sea, past this or that obstacle, allergy, danger-sign, to her own Personality, so that she emerges, not as a mere appendage to some other human being—a Charley's Aunt, a Pharoah's Daughter, a Whistler's Mother, but, uniquely, Herself.

What happens to a specialist? From personal observation I would say that she contrives progressively, and from an early age, to know more and more about less and less until at length she brings forth a degree, a doctorate, a directorship, or some other utterly un-hatchable egg, completely useless as the nucleus of a home, and spends the rest of her available span in a slightly peevish prosperity.

Obviously, here, activity and application have been excessive, which according to Bertrand Russell is fatal to happiness.

Give her a career by all means, but make it one with a far horizon—the care of children or animals, who are different every day and for ever. Some earthy occupation such as gardening or rat-catching, or watching the seasons swallowing each other's tails in endless procession on a farm. That's a job with eternity in it if you like!

Let her make chairs or cheese, iron gates, or beer-barrels, or wedding cakes, or funeral wreaths. Let her follow any of the arts or crafts or humanities. It doesn't so much matter what the career is so long as it's not *just* a career, there should be something creative about it which gives it, and her, a reason for existing and an ideal of perfection at which to aim.

Preferably it should be something in which men do not compete.

Perhaps some unfortunate economic necessity arises and she is obliged to sing for her supper, or if the poor child has no voice, type for her lunch. But as the highest post open to women is that of a wife and mother it seems to me wasteful of good material to let her take on a job a man could do just as well.

Man is a poor fish when it comes to raising babies and cooking for his family (though I *did* once know one who poached the most miraculous eggs). It is therefore better to let the sons go to the offices and the daughters (though fully aware that they could do both jobs with one hand tied behind them) make joyful their return.

You may also have detected some personal bias in this "career" theme. The fact is that the specialists, the careerists, have escaped from us.

We, as their mothers, are left behind once their soaring

wings bear them away to Higher Things. We can't keep pace with them, flap we never so wildly, because they are treading pastures we never knew.

They will still be kind to us of course. But they can't help being condescending, and a pat on the head from some patronising, lofty beings with whom we now have no tie except by the accident of birth—no mutual sympathies—no interchangeable ideas, is not among the greater joys of Parenthood.

X

Emotions? Well, why not?

"It is extraordinary how many emotional storms one may
weather in safety, if one is ballasted with ever so little gold."
William McFee.

ADOLESCENT emotions are likely at times to render our
companionable progress more like a dog fight than a
peaceful saunter. But I don't really blame the child. She's in a
No-man's Land between school and home, childhood and the
adult state—nothing is charted or certain, not even herself, her
wants, her capabilities. Is it any wonder that at times her
bewilderment boils over into excessive affection or hatred,
desires for love or revenge.

Your function is to sympathise with these emotions. It's
all you can do. Just sympathise and stick around. If she feels

that there is something solid behind the chaos it will be a rock to which she can cling in times of storm.

Interests hitherto have been largely turned outwards, but as The Child grows up they turn inward. Waves of gloom and introspection may sweep her. Alternate wild dissipation and depression; religion and abandon, turn her into a schizophrenic and it's your job to keep pace with her. Does she weep, then weep with her. She wants to drink? Then drink with her. Weave garlands of metaphorical flowers with her and be ready at any time to applaud, condole, confer, congratulate, cheer, or abscond with her. It's all part of her dizzy progress.

It's a trying time for one and all but need not be devastating. And it's no personal misfortune, merely a sign that she's growing up.

A parent is a safety-valve for boiling-over emotions.

Feelings are there to be expressed. When and how she will express them is largely a matter of what outlets you offer.

Let her think for you and protect you. Explain the world to you. Advise on your clothes and make-up (a subject on which her knowledge is likely to be exhaustive and her efforts creative). If she takes over the job of making a new woman of you she won't have time for much destructive emotion, it's the girl with time on her hands who becomes bored and bad.

Perhaps you don't *want* to be made over? Never mind, she can always take up painting, fashion designing, needlework or hairdressing, from an abstract, rather than a personal, point of view and it will do her just as much good. Though the results won't be so interesting, or so beneficial to yourself.

Her habits are as fascinating to study as those of wild animals. Indeed pro. tem. she *is* a wild animal and one can only deduce from her actions what is going on in her mind. But never question her directly about her troubles, just let

her talk while you listen. You will hear it all in good time, and in helping her to be happy you will *both* be happy. The cultivation of the emotions is a much neglected art and now is a good time for you to get some practice.

The riches of the human soul are all but indestructible. Fed and led in the right way the power they engender will move mountains. But by constant curbing, denigration, ridicule, they can in time be so atrophied and astringed that they vanish without trace, as if they had never been.

Why in heaven's name we cultivate carefully all the other senses and stamp on our delicate feelings is beyond my comprehension.

From the time when The Child first cries at the pictures, gets a crush on the sports-mistress, or goes dewy-eyed over a film star, she is taught that any display of emotion is ridiculous, unworthy, and in downright bad taste.

You tell her to "control" her emotions by which you mean "eradicate" them and if she can't do so you behave as if they were a corpse under the parquet and pretend they're not there, though paling a little now and then as you get a stronger whiff.

Let them out into the air, lady, and they won't smell.

What if she *does* giggle? A giggle is often the only outlet for her over-charged emotion.

What if her rages are cyclonic and unpredictable? It is a form of affection as well as a valuable safety valve. Let it rip, and at the same time be thankful that she vents it on *you*. It's an honour really, and, if you look at it the right way, an additional interest in your middle-aged life.

Ever been in a small sailing boat on a squally day? It's bewildering and bruising. You never know whether you'll be on the crest or in the trough of the wave, in sunshine or bitter showers, in a dead calm or half dead with a blow from a swinging boom. You've got to be prepared for anything and resent nothing, but it's exciting all right, once you get your sea legs. So is this daughter business.

Emotions aren't unpleasant things to have, so long as they're in proportion to the rest of her life. The cultivation of emotion and sensory perceptions in general is just as valuable as history and geography. They are aids to harmonious living and a gateway into a better world, through which many things will be made known to her that she could never learn from teachers.

Reeling, writhing and fainting in coils may not be usual items in adolescent education but these and other emotional accomplishments have their part in developing her sensitivity, enriching her personality and releasing, to the full, unsuspected potentialities. You can accompany her in this giddy programme in many directions.

"If the ship be troubled with rats," said my great-grandfather's Manual of Standard Seamanship, "place a good deal of dry newspapers in the sail locker for the rats to chew on."

But you needn't stop at chewing dry newspapers.

Explore together the endless avenues of music, painting, the play, poetry and the deeper kind of book—the whole celestial vista. You may make an artist of her or she may make one of you. Or neither.

But in encouraging and *evoking* her emotions, instead of stamping on them, you will surmount together such snags as arise in the pilgrimage.

And the dual surmounting of snags is a very powerful cement in any human relationship.

Sensitivity is just as important to the young as book-learning and a better aid to living, making of the happy possessor a delicate instrument, receptive of every passing impression. Moreover it is a tricky thing to guide and to develop. Nourish and feed it carefully, encourage its tentative explorations and let it never fear rebuffs. You may yet have a genius in the family if she can feel right down to her finger-tips, every sensation that ever touches her.

Emotion is the power of deriving pleasure from external objects and is a function of the entire personality, embracing senses, reactions and mental awareness. It is our response to life, and though it may be creative or destructive, exhilarating or depressing, it can never be boring or ignored. Only by cultivating the full range of her emotions will she be living and expressing herself fully.

Never lose patience and never, never snub her, even if for the moment you can't think what she's up to.

Good daughters, before now, have left home, soured and hardened, for uncongenial jobs because their adolescent emotions were stamped upon or dismissed as bad taste. You must be prepared to hop over to the other side of the counter and see how things look from *her* point of view. Project your feelings across the gap between you and visualise her difficulties. Don't expect to establish good relations with her merely by being a good mother. If you're *too* good, too *ostentatiously* good she'll hate you for it.

Quite right too. Mothercraft is the supreme case for hiding lights under bushels, and unless you play down *your* side of the partnership and play up hers she will do her crying on someone else's shoulder. Study *her* likes and dislikes, don't necessarily assume that she should adopt *yours*. After all, she grew that way, as a carrot does, to adapt herself to conditions in the world around her. It's a waste of effort on both sides to try cramming her into some other mould, and will result in permanent damage.

So love her—listen to her—understand her—encourage her to play the whole range of her moods as if they were a piano.

It may sound stormy at times.

All the better, you know then that none of the notes are mute. But if she has no love, no warmth, no passions, then she may be as clever as an electric computer or a Russian nuclear scientist but I wouldn't give a fig for her chance of happiness.

XI

Yes, My Darling Daughter

"Fair is youth and free of sorrow
Yet how soon its joys we bury
Let who would be, now be merry
Sure is no-one of tomorrow."
            Old Song

THIS IS going to be an annoying chapter for mothers, a kind of Freedom Charter for the Female Young and will be most unscientific.

If you don't like this it's unfortunate but immovable. I have my own sense of the rightness and wrongness of the world, and that's the way it must go, take it or leave it.

Since the first mother replied to the she-child's demand, with the classic answer (so limited in a literal sense but infinite in its implications) in the poem:

"Mother may I go out to swim?
Yes, my darling daughter,
Leave your clothes right on the brim
And don't go near the water."

has seemed to cover most phases of the mother/daughter relationship.

The girl was admittedly out of date, she actually *asked* permission for this exercise in natation, instead of calling out as she swung down the stairs "I've taken your new Sea-Sports swimsuit, mamma, and pinched Pop's petrol. See you some time. Bye-ee-ee", leaving you to fill in the gaps for yourself.

I think she was a *nice* child and her mother did well to return an unhesitating affirmative.

She was obliged (being aware, by reason of her greater years and experience, of wolves who lurk under gooseberries [or is that storks] and on lidos) to qualify the permission slightly. But provided that Daughter kept her eyes open (which you'd need to do with no clothes on and nowhere near any water) it was O.K. with mamma.

Risks are a part of growing up and of character formation, but once she's aware of them let her go close enough to sniff at them, like going right up to all the jumps and seeing what they're made of before you tackle a steeplechase.

The world is her book. If she reads it incorrectly she must be blinded by either passion, pride, resentment or sheer pig-headedness. And you, madam, should explain and display its varied pleasures to her as if she were entering a convent tomorrow and hadn't a moment to lose.

So having taught her to read this book and imbibe knowledge from it, you must allow her the opportunity to put her knowledge into practice. The sooner she learns to tumble the sooner she will learn to pick herself up. The delights of liberty and free choice outweigh by far the pain of bruises. There may be tears, but there will be more laughter, and as the experience and discrimination increase, the need for outside aid, First Aid, or any other aid, disappears.

I don't say that she will never hurt either herself or you. She will. But she may do a great deal of *damage* without doing *wrong*. It's only wrong if she *meant* it to be wrong. The intention is the important thing, not the hasty destructive action which is no worse than that of a blundering puppy.

Therefore, having, through the early years, contrived that her education is as negative as possible (but that she is free from vice and wrong intentions, with only one commandment, "Never hurt anybody"), you can let her loose for some practice.

You observe that the mother of the would-be bather didn't say "Promise me you won't go near the water" (it would have made the line the wrong length anyway). And when the child returned I'll bet you half my royalties that her mother wasn't waiting up with the air of a martyr to say, "Where have you been and with whom?"

Never demand the truth, lest they are tempted to conceal it, and never a promise, lest they are obliged to break it.

Leave them alone, I tell you.

Whether there are wolves in the wood, sharks in the carmarket, hogs on the road or other curiosities of natural history in her path, let her meet them, knowing that they exist, and develop her own resistance.

The weapons with which to overcome hazards must, like beauty and the ability to wring tunes from a trumpet, come from inside of her, not out.

She must have money for these adventures naturally, preferably her own allowance, from the time she can have her own banking account. It will teach her how to apportion it and make it last—What are the enduring things, but dull, and what (such as orchids for mothers) are a blazing joy on which to blue one's cash, if of a slightly evanescent nature.

It is learning relative values by her own trials and errors which is going to keep her by your side, reporting the result of her experiments and occasionally borrowing a shoulder to cry on if they go wrong, but always ready for more.

Let her carry on, even if it means coming another cropper. Better break the child's neck than her spirit.

Don't keep her on a lead.

If she wants to drive her sports car at eighty, let her. It is the quickest way for her to learn that virtuosity in a car, as on a piano, is more a question of sensitivity, practice and keeping your mind on your job, than of hoggish display with one eye on the audience and the other on the clock.

And don't insist on accompanying her to make sure that she doesn't "go near the water". On the other hand, if she momentarily runs out of friends and throws you a casual invitation be ready to drop everything and go.

Believe me it's an honour.

But hang on to your hat.

Let her be the judge of what is good for her. How can you expect her to know her safe capacity for speed, drink, late nights and excitement if she's never tried them?

Does she drink? Of course she does. She's had wine with her meals since she was nine and now has an unconscious palate and a discrimination which is the quiet admiration of

the Aged. But she doesn't drink too much. She appreciates drink for what it *is* and *has*, rather than for what it *does* and is far beyond any such bravado as boasting of the amount she can carry.

I put alcohol first, because, that lesson learned, she is ready for the next, which is boys, and the same principles apply.

To keep the wolf from the door she's got to recognize a wolf when she sees one and be handy with a whiff of wolf-destroyer if needed.

She knows all about them and is used to handling them and sorting them out from the harmless necessary flock of boy friends. There's no danger of these going to her head, because however attractive they may be, like drink, she knows where to stop. Therefore there is nothing but pleasure and benefit in the association.

What's the good of all this modern instruction on the relationship between the sexes if it has to come solely from books?

You can't *teach* relationship, *any* relationship. You have to *feel* it, slowly, hesitantly, advancing and retreating, putting forth one delicate feeler after another. And for pity's sake don't hedge her about with restrictions, so that she never gets a chance of making boy friends at all.

If you are sufficiently encouraging in this respect she will treat you as a confidante and even possibly upon occasion ask your advice. A new and delightful sympathy will ripen between you, entirely because she feels you're tackling this boy friend business together.

Encourage her to go to mixed parties. And no hard and fast stipulations about the hour of return. You may *suggest* but not demand.

Curfews are stupid mediaeval measures. If a girl is bent on going off the rails she's as likely to do it before midnight as after. And to know that recriminations await her late arrival will probably induce her to try it on, just to see the effect.

If the way (and the front door) is wide open and she knows that she can't create an effect by returning at some chilly scandalous hour, it won't be worth her while to prolong her petting party unduly.

She'd really rather be in bed but, if opposed in this matter of late hours, will continue it till she drops asleep on her feet, rather than admit that you're right.

Once you realise that ninety-nine per cent of all naughtiness is an attempt to project her personality—to build up a commodity which as yet is somewhat jellified and nothing much to hold on to, you can get close to her and match every step she takes. You know that even the fierce storms that occasionally arise are only a sign of the fierce affection of a sensitive child, so why not ignore them?

She is obliged to produce a defence against her very youthfulness and uncertainty and if it means being a shade over-assertive at times, it is an error of judgement, rather than an error of taste.

At this semi-final, or "fully-fledged" stage someone is sure to talk glibly about "youth at the helm". If I knew which end of the darn boat the helm *was* (if either) I would be prepared to discourse more fully on it.

It seems to me that with both boats and daughters (being feminine) you are up against more than meets the eye.

And, in any case, might it not be possible to steer her from behind?

I am told that in the whole of Nature and Mechanics there is no such thing as a *pull*. It's all *push*. I can almost hear you objecting violently and talking about horses pulling carts.

But *do* they?

I have examined the subject in great detail, inconvenience, and indeed apprehension, at certain stages and close quarters, and the facts are thus:

The scientists have undoubtedly *got* something.

The horse couldn't do a thing about pulling if there weren't a loop on his harness up by his back end, which, being slid over a hook on the cart, *pushes* hook, cart and everything. The horse is apparently there only by accident and tradition. It is the same with any moving object. If available I have verified these. If not, *not*.

But it does occur to me that despite what is said about youth guiding and leading us, it is possible that the pull is purely an illusion and the push is coming from further back, out of sight and out of mind. So let us neither praise nor blame them for what may not be their doing.

In any case it's a co-operative movement between the two ends, the results of a gentleman's agreement to go in the same direction at the same time.

This is called the March of Progress and has been going on ever since there *was* any Time but not really getting anywhere.

It is demonstrated vividly in hackney displays at horse shows, in which the moving object performs violent and frequently picturesque movements vertically, while the earth lazily continues its customary revolutions horizontally. It does no one any harm and is good for the liver and relieving boredom.

If we are getting anywhere at all with this chapter (which I doubt) it is towards a conclusion that progress is illusion— however much noise the young make and however fast they appear to be, that too is an illusion, an algebraic problem concerning the difference between your pace and theirs, your angle of view and whichever is the slower shall deem that the other is the faster, and it's all rather absurd.

There are other axioms for onlookers to which I hope you will pay uncommon attention. Such as:

Don't panic, it may never happen.

A miss is as good as a mile.

Don't cry over spilt milk.

Least said soonest mended.

There's safety in numbers.

A still tongue makes a wise head.

More haste less speed.

Age quod agis (this is Latin and means "Look what *you're* doing you poor mutt, and let the others look after themselves".) Very cute and snappy and should be embroidered on every mother's blazer pocket, surrounding a crest of a goose and a mule both rampant and two capital L's both proper.

And if any downcast and defeated daughter desires information on how to keep pace with her mamma she should apply immediately.

I have, in my time, been both.